GROWING UP
God
WITH

GROWING UP God WITH

How God Gave Me My Own Bible Story

BEVERLEY JOHNSON

Unless otherwise indicated, scripture quotations are taken from the Holy Bible, King James Version, which is in the public domain. • Scripture quotations marked (NKJV) are taken from the New King James Version®. Copyright © 1982 by Thomas Nelson, Inc. Used by permission. All rights reserved. • Scripture quotations marked (NLT) are taken from the Holy Bible, New Living Translation, copyright ©1996, 2004, 2007 by Tyndale House Foundation. Used by permission of Tyndale House Publishers, Inc., Carol Stream, Illinois 60188. All rights reserved.

Softcover ISBN: 978-1-4866-2443-0
Hardcover ISBN: 978-1-4866-2657-1
eBook ISBN: 978-1-4866-2444-7

Word Alive Press
119 De Baets Street Winnipeg, MB R2J 3R9
www.wordalivepress.ca

WORD ALIVE
—P R E S S—

Cataloguing in Publication information can be obtained from Library and Archives Canada.

To Christa and Mekaylah.

CONTENTS

CHAPTER ONE

The Day Jesus Came out of the Bible

It was around six o'clock in the morning when I was awakened suddenly from my sleep. I felt the strong presence of *The Man*—in the room—again. Cussing under my breath, I yanked the sheet off my head. Instinctively, my gaze was drawn, as if by magnets, in the direction of my feet, where I felt, or rather sensed, his presence. Instead of the usual empty space, I saw tiny fragments of light shimmering in the space between my sister's bed and mine. Fascinated, I remained transfixed, eyes wide open, wondering what those dancing lights could be. I stared in amazement as the lights slowly began to coalesce into the shape of—

"Jesus!" I shouted.

Smiling, Jesus put his index finger to his lips, as if to say, "Shh."

I looked across the room and saw my sister still sleeping on her bed, which was perpendicular to mine, forming an L-shape. Jesus was standing between both beds, at the side of mine and the foot of hers, wearing clothing from his time period on Earth—a dark reddish-orange tunic or the loose garment worn over clothing shown in pictures of Jesus and people from that culure and time period, draped over a cream-coloured garment.

I lowered my voice. "Jesus, are you really here? In my room?"

I looked at him standing there, smiling at me as if to say, "See for yourself."

It was too good to be true.

"Nice dream," I said to Jesus and myself as I pulled the sheet over my head to go back to sleep. I removed the sheets again to take another look. Jesus was still standing there, waiting patiently for me.

"You're still here? Is this really happening? Jesus, is it really you?"

He moved from my feet toward my face and stopped in the middle of the room, where there was more space. He held out His hands for me to see the holes where the nails had pierced them.

"Oh, you didn't have to do that. I know it's you. It's just that nothing good ever happens to me," I said.

I knew it was Jesus. His eyes radiated so much love and warmth. There was so much love and peace—joy even—in the room. I saw love; I felt love—overwhelming love. I just knew it was Jesus, but I couldn't believe he was *here*—with me! Out of the Bible, down from heaven. It was the *me* part that I was having a problem with.

"Okay, I know it's you, Jesus. But why are you here? Am I dead?"

"No, you're not dead."

"Am I dreaming?"

"No, you're not dreaming."

"Then I don't get it. You? Me? In this room? At the same time? But … but … but nothing good ever happens to me."

Jesus walked over to my bedside and stood in front of me. He was about to say something, but I spoke before he could begin. "Jesus, could you please just stand here so I can keep looking at you?" I just wanted to look at him, to savour his presence. He moved closer and stood still. I looked at him for a good while.

By his body language and facial expression, I knew that he thought I'd looked at him long enough. He indicated that he was there for a reason. Then he gazed upward at the ceiling, looking through it toward the sky with rapid eye movements. I sensed it was a form of communication and concluded that the sun was talking to him, telling him the day was quickly breaking and that he had to hurry back to heaven. I may have gotten that idea from the biblical story of Jacob wrestling with the angel.

Jesus turned and looked me straight in the eyes and said, "Go abroad and feed God's children."

I replied with a smile. It had been my dream since childhood to build a big house and then go about collecting all the unwanted and neglected children, who I believed were God's children, so I could take care of them by providing a loving home with lots of food to eat and nice clothes to wear. I looked at Jesus with a *you're-kidding-me-right?* look. I figured he knew all about my dream to be the mother of an orphanage, and that I had no money to get it started. I thought he was just pulling my leg, so to speak. But he wasn't kidding. He was very serious, and he was waiting for me to respond.

By that time I was sitting up in bed. I opened my hands and replied, "Jesus, I don't have any money!"

He gave me an I'm-trying-not-to-crack-up-here smile. Then, taking me completely off-guard, he began to sing a new verse to the hymn, "There Were Ninety and Nine."

While he sang, I laughed because I recognized the song as my song, and I didn't know he could sing. "Jesus, you do go to church!" He had to go to church regularly to know that song and to know that it was my favourite song to sing to myself in church. When no adult was around, I would search for that hymn in the hymnal and sing it quietly to myself while my friends and siblings played.

"Jesus, you can sing, man."

No one ever told me Jesus could sing. There's no mention of him singing in the Bible, and it never crossed my mind that he could, or would, sing. I always pictured him preaching, teaching, praying, and even weeping, but never singing. When Jesus finished singing, he looked up toward heaven, or rather through the roof, with the same rapid eye movement, as if communicating with someone. Then he said, "Repeat after me."

One line at a time, He recited the words of the new verse he had just sung, and I repeated each line after him. When he got to the end of the verse he said, "Now *you* sing it by yourself."

"Jesus, I can't sing a whole verse after repeating it once after you. I don't know the words. You have to teach it to me some more."

"Try singing it anyway."

I opened my mouth to sing, and to my amazement, the words rolled off my tongue. I was laughing as I sang, astonished that I was singing an entire verse that I didn't know the words to. I remember thinking how neat it would be if new information worked that way between my teachers and I at school.

When I finished singing, Jesus said, "I have to go now."

I burst into tears. "Please, don't go yet. Stay with me longer."

He had already moved over to the wall, closer to the door. I looked him up and down, still crying, and asked him to stay with me some more. He stayed there for a while so I could look at him a little longer. Then he said, "I really have to go now," and he turned to leave.

Just then, I wondered if Jesus knew that despite his visit, I wasn't going to stay in church. The Bible says Jesus can hear your thoughts, so I wondered if he could really hear my thoughts. I had started going back to church a few months earlier, after leaving Sunday school several years before that. Now, after much wrestling in my mind, I decided to leave again to go back to the nightclubs and the movies.

At that instant, Jesus turned and looked at me. He walked toward me, stopped directly in front of me, and said, "Look at me."

By then I was sitting up in bed. I stopped crying and looked into his eyes. He pointed a finger at my eye, and then his eyes started doing that rapid eye movement thing again as he looked deeply into mine. I felt something somewhere deep inside my stomach area unwinding like a movie reel. When he withdrew his finger, the reel stopped. It restarted when he pointed his finger at my eye again. He did this a total of three times, as if searching for something in my past, or perhaps in my future. The first two times he did this, I got the impression that he didn't like what he saw. The third time, he looked a bit more relieved, but still not too thrilled.

He moved backward, closer to the wall, looking at me with what I felt was a mixture of empathy, compassion, and great concern. He looked to the sky again, as if asking if there was anything he should say to me, or for some measure of assurance that I would be okay despite my decision to not remain in church. I assumed Jesus was communicating with his Father in heaven. The Bible often says that he "lifted up his eyes to Heaven" when speaking to God, so I assumed he was either talking to God, who is way up in heaven, or perhaps to the sun, which I believed kept reminding him it was time to go, though I wanted him to stay.

Jesus raised his hand to say goodbye to me and to say, "I'm ready" to the sun. Up to that point, I hadn't seen any light, just fragments of light. The sun's presence was an impression or feeling I had. "Bev, I really have to go now, but there's one thing I want to leave with you: *There is only one way.*"

Just then, an enormous beam of light shot out from what appeared to be the sun and enveloped him. It seemed to transform him into his heavenly body. His clothes remained the same, but he appeared to be transparent. Still, I was too fascinated by the brightness of the sun and its beam to take it all in. The beam from the sun was so bright that it penetrated the walls of the room and caused them to disappear, so I could clearly see outside into the yard and the sky above. I could see the sun hovering some distance above, just over the gate near the skinny ackee tree. The beam flooded the entire area from the sun to the room.

Sitting up in bed, I watched as Jesus ascended into heaven in the beam. He was travelling so fast, I won't even attempt to describe or calculate his speed, as I never imagined that rate of movement was possible. At times it seemed as if he and the light were travelling in slow motion, but the increasing height of the sun as it ascended in the sky made me realize they were moving way too fast for my brain to compute. I sat on the bed, looking up into the skies, eyes and mouth open wide in amazement, and thinking, *I had no idea the sky was so high.* He continued to ascend ever upward until I could see the sun, the beam, and Jesus going up, up, up all the way into the heavens, which were constantly parting upward beyond my wildest imagination. The end of the beam remained over the gate and the ackee tree.

As I watched Jesus ascend higher and higher, I realized that I might never have another encounter with Him or be so happy again in this life. I took quick stock of my life and decided that I didn't have much to gain by staying here on this planet. I wondered if I could still catch up with Jesus and go home with him. The light disappeared and the walls of the room returned. I jumped off the bed and made a run for the door. I quickly turned the doorknob, but the door was locked with the key still in it. I turned the key, opened the door, and ran outside, hoping to catch the beam and get beamed up into the sun. I wanted to go home to heaven, right after Jesus.

Once outside, I saw that the beam was gone. I was angry. The sun stared at me with its usual look of indifference. "Why did you take your beam up and leave me here? Don't look all innocent. You know what I'm talking about." I stood there, accusing the sun of denying me the privilege of ascending into heaven with Jesus, until it dawned on me that even though I couldn't go with Jesus, he was on his way up and would tell God about me. *At last! Finally!* God was going to know I existed, and things would start to change for me.

Jesus was going to give an account of what he did on Earth that morning. He was going to say, "Father, I went where you sent me and did what you told me to do. However, on my way back, I made an unscheduled stop at Bev's house…"

Then God would ask Him, "Who is Bev, and where is she from?"

And Jesus would point to my house and show God who I was. God would look down from heaven and finally know that I existed, and he'd want to know more about me.

I started to do my God-knows-me dance—a happy dance I invented when I was a little girl. I'd been saving it for the day I had proof that God knew me, and this was the day. *But what if Jesus is still on his way up?* I didn't want to do my crazy dance before God knew me. I wanted God to see me dancing. So I waited a bit and then told myself, *he must be there by now. God is looking down at me now. Now dance like crazy!* Staring up at the sun, I danced until I was exhausted.

Then it suddenly occurred to me that it would be very embarrassing if the neighbours saw me out in the yard dancing so early in the morning without any music, just me staring up into the sky and dancing like a madwoman. They'd think I had totally lost my mind. If they asked for an explanation and I told them the truth, it would only confirm that I had gone completely off my rocker. I looked around timidly to see if anyone was watching from a window or anywhere else. Luckily, I saw no one, and no one saw me. Whew! No puzzled looks, raised eyebrows, or questions from the neighbours to respond to in order to justify my wild, crazy dancing.

With mixed feelings of relief, joy, anger, and sadness, I returned to the house. Relief because no one saw me staring up into the sky and doing that silly dance without music. Sad and angry because I'd lost time fussing with the door to get outside, and the sun had taken up its giant beam of light before I could get to it. Happy, happy, happy that God finally knew me.

My sister, Merna, was still fast asleep in bed. I can't recall if I woke her up to tell her that Jesus had been there and she'd slept through it all. We weren't on speaking terms, but my excitement might have caused me to forget all of that, wake her up, and blurt out what had just happened. If I did, she'd just think I'd had a nice dream, and she'd go right back to sleep.

But I couldn't go back to sleep, so I sat pondering the enormity of what had just taken place. Then I recalled Jesus's instruction that I should go abroad and feed God's children. In that moment, it was revealed that I was supposed to feed them by writing books. *Oh, you want me to go abroad and write books for little children in North America who think Christmas and Easter are about Santa Claus and a bunny rabbit?* I thought to myself. *Sure, I can write little Ladybird-like books for children. I will give one the title* The Real Meaning of Christmas *and the other* The Real Meaning of Easter. Ladybird books are a popular children's book series from the UK that I loved reading in primary school.

Then I said out loud, "Jesus, I owe you an apology for locking you out of my life. I don't know why I locked you out, but I know that I did, and I am so sorry." Whenever I'd thought about heaven in the past, I only thought about God and the angel Gabriel; I never thought of Jesus until that day.

As I sang the verse Jesus had taught me, I got up and set about doing my chores. I sang it over and over, still thinking how great it would've been had I been able to learn so easily from my teachers at school. Then suddenly, as if by magic, the first line vanished from my memory. I thought it strange, but try as I might, I couldn't recall it. I remembered the other lines and continued to sing them. Then the second line disappeared, and

I could only sing the rest. One by one, the lines all disappeared, until the whole verse was gone. As I now recall, so too did the command to "Go abroad and feed God's children." I vividly remembered Jesus's visit, his presence, and the brightness of what I referred to as the sun. Its light and beam never faded. But most of what he said to me disappeared and remained hidden for some time.

I was expecting my best friend, Dolsie, to stop by the house soon. It was our usual routine doing odd jobs because we didn't have money to continue our education: she would call for me around ten o'clock each morning on her way to her cousin Hyacinth's house, where we would pass the time playing cards or dominoes. I was bursting with excitement, and I could hardly wait for her to arrive. I saw her coming and went to meet her in the yard.

"Guess who was here this morning," I said to her excitedly as she got closer to me. Reading the joy in my voice and the happiness written all over my face, she started guessing the names of guys I liked, or who liked me, or guys we'd met in the nightclubs or at the movies.

"Is it D—?"

"No!"

"C—?

"Nope!"

"J—?"

"No!"

Knowing she would never guess the right answer, I said, "It was Jesus! Jesus came to see me this morning." Still very happy and excited, I tried to recount all that had happened, including how I couldn't recall the words to the verse of the song Jesus had taught me, because the lines had vanished one by one from my memory. I couldn't tell her the part where he told me to go abroad and feed God's children, because that too was gone from my memory.

She listened intently and then looked me in the eye and in a serious voice said, "Bev, do you know what this means? It means you can't go to nightclubs and parties anymore. You have to stay in church. God is calling you."

I gave her a look that wasn't very nice. "No, it doesn't mean that. Jesus was just passing through Jamaica and made a stop at my house. God's not calling me." I couldn't grasp, and maybe deep down didn't want to believe, that Jesus had come from heaven just to see me, and that he did so for a specific reason.

I justified his visit by reasoning that he had been sent to aid a righteous person in Jamaica who needed immediate help. On his way back to heaven, he came across my prayers going up to God for help. Since he was in the area, he decided to come see the person who had sent up so many prayers. He was going to tell God about me, and things were going to be fine from now on.

After Jesus left that morning, I started researching his words as recorded in the Bible. He and his words came alive to me. But I couldn't give up the night life, and it wasn't long until my encounter with Jesus was replaced with dancing, listening to the latest hit songs, and my preoccupation with the latest fashion. I returned to dancing and having a good time with Dolsie and our friends in the nightclubs and at house parties. But it wasn't the same. Something had changed. The music just didn't hit me the way it used to, and when I danced, my legs felt as if something was holding on to them, forcing me to fight to make them move. I couldn't glide across the dance floor or gyrate as before.

Dolsie turned to me one evening on our way to May Pen, where the movie theatre and nightclubs were, and said, "Why did you stop going to church? I was about to join you there." Her revelation left me with even more guilt for being so weak and leaving church. If I'd known Dolsie was thinking of joining me in church, I would have stayed. I thought she was having more fun than I, and I missed dressing up and going out dancing. Still, we partied on, the backslider and the almost persuaded, and I continued reading the Bible and praying each night, or I should say early morning, when I got home from the movies, nightclubs, and parties.

The old cowboy movies of my primary school days had now given way to colourful depictions of Black American lives. Movies such as *Claudine*, *Cotton Comes to Harlem*, *The Autobiography of Miss Jane Pitman*, just to name a few, opened my eyes to the reality of life in the USA, but I was still determined to get there.

During this time, I had a major problem that had been going on for about four or five years, and that only God could solve. It was a problem so big that it was a matter of life and death. It had me praying and reading my Bible morning and night. Problem: Out of this world. Cause: Unknown. Symptoms: Invisible, but I very much felt "burnings" that can't fully or adequately be described with words.

The morning Jesus came out of the Bible, my plan, after pulling the sheet off my head, had been to move over to my sister's bed, where she lay sleeping, and try to sleep on the side closest to the wall, where I felt safer and less exposed. That's because I was being "burned" by someone I referred to as "The Man." My sister was a bad sleeper who tossed and turned in her sleep. She tended to throw her legs and arms about while sleeping. She'd have her hand in my face and her leg across my abdomen. I don't like anyone close to me when I'm sleeping. We hadn't been on speaking terms for quite some time, so we usually ended up arguing about why I would leave an empty bed to come pick a fight with her.

I kept my Bible open at all times on the dinner tray table at my head for divine protection from evil. But that didn't prevent the burnings, so I slept with my head at the foot of the bed, keeping my head close to the door and the windows. The house consisted of only two rooms, and sleeping that way made it easier for me to run out of the house during the day. But that morning, I had no need to try to climb into bed beside my sister or run outside. I say "try" because most of the time something or someone would zap or touch me, and I'd be unable to move anything but my eyes. But that morning I felt safe. I felt happy. I felt loved. I felt and tasted love.

Allow me to take you back in time to the events leading up to that morning and why I was cussing and uttering threats at The Man. Over the years, things had gone from bad to worse in my home financially, and I got used to living with poverty and disappointment. Things had gotten so bad that I was forced to drop out of school before my fourteenth birthday. That was a very traumatic experience for me, because I loved school and did well there. I wanted to be with kids in my age group at Denbigh

Junior Secondary School, doing what they were doing: learning, planning the future, and having fun being silly and carefree. To protect my mind, I told myself to stop expecting good things to happen and just take each day as it came.

The day I dropped out of school was the day The Man dropped into my life. I had never seen him, but after some time, I concluded that he was very intelligent, so he must be a spirit. I also sensed he was a man. In fact, the day I came to that conclusion, I shouted, "I know who you are!" I knew that I knew him, but I just couldn't put my finger on the name. After spending some time trying to figure out who he was, I gave up and yelled, "You are a man… and you are a spirit!" So much for knowing who he was. I prayed and begged for help to get back into school, and all I got was that presence. Well, that and the burnings that followed my every attempt to escape him.

What I'd come to refer to as burnings felt more like being zapped by electricity or a laser. As soon as I sensed my environment become extraordinarily quiet, I knew The Man was present, and I'd try to run, but something like electricity would hit me and I'd become paralyzed. My survival instincts would take over and I'd fight, cuss, yell, or scream—but to no avail. No one ever heard me. I'd lose consciousness for about fifteen minutes and then reawaken to the intense burning sensations inside my body, especially my joints.

So that morning when I first felt him looking at me from the foot of my bed, I thought he was there to "burn" me again. I opened my eyes and stared at the spot where I sensed the strong presence. Under the blankets, I was cussing, saying, among other things, *Leave me alone! Leave me alone! Why won't you leave me alone? What do you want from me? What do you want from me? Why are you bothering me?* I yelled in my mind, something I did every time I felt his presence.

Although he remained unseen, I always sensed him. I even covered myself from head to toe with a blanket in a vain attempt to protect myself from him as I slept, just in case he showed up while I was deep in sleep.

The burnings occurred most often at night just before I fell asleep and early in the mornings before I got up. The Man showed up as soon as the last person in the room fell asleep. I'm a light sleeper, and from as early as I can remember, I've had a hard time falling asleep. Worrying about The Man showing up to burn me didn't help my attempts to close my eyes, rest, and sleep peacefully. Even in the daytime I'd feel his presence, no matter where I was.

The main requirement for him to be present seemed to be for me to be alone. If I was babysitting, he'd leave just before the child awoke. If someone were coming to visit, he'd leave just before the person arrived. That's why I concluded he was a spirit. He was intelligent. He knew things before I did. Epilepsy or other forms of illness didn't leave because another human was near and then return when it was convenient to do so. Distraught, angry, afraid, and questioning my sanity, I was fighting for my life against something or someone I could neither see nor escape. I knew there was nothing inappropriate happening, and that I wasn't being abused, but the presence was still very powerful.

I can't say where or if he touched me, because I never felt a touch, but my limbs became paralyzed from his burn. If I were sitting or lying down with a book, my eyes would begin to feel heavy, and I'd feel the need to put the book down and take a break. After putting the book down, I'd sense his presence and get up to run out of the room. And that's when he would zap me. My attempts to leave the room were futile. Except for my eyes, I couldn't move a muscle, and no one ever heard my screams for help. Knowing that no one would respond to my plight, I'd start calling on God for help.

"God! God! Please help me! Please come to my rescue and save me from this man!" I'd yell and scream. In desperation, I'd begin praying the Lord's Prayer or the Shepherd's Psalm while going under. I was afraid to die, and I wasn't sure if I'd regain consciousness, so I fought with all my might, cussing and praying, to keep from going under, but to no avail. I'd look around the room but see no one. Then I'd feel myself slip into unconsciousness, my body sinking into the mattress, and another part of me floating or flying upward toward the sky. The last thing I'd see before losing consciousness would be my nose looming before my eyes. I was usually unconscious for about fifteen minutes.

If the "burning" happened at night or early in the morning, then I had no choice but to lie in bed, praying and cussing until I fell asleep. If it happened during the day, I would flee out the door like someone escaping death. My survival instincts alone helped me make it as far as the set of concrete blocks that comprised our makeshift steps at the door, as my legs had no strength and my entire body felt as though it was on fire, burning from the inside out. I later realized that my resistance to the Holy Spirit was the source of my pain.

There I'd sit, breathing through my mouth because I was exhausted and to cool my body down faster so I could regain my strength and go off to Hya's house. While waiting, I'd stare at the sun, crying, "God, God, see what happens to someone when you don't care about them? When are you going come to my aid?" I'd been praying, crying, and pleading with God to get rid of The Man, who I thought was a ghost or demon intent on killing me. Once the burning would stop, my strength would gradually return and I'd be free to move about again.

My first instinct was always to get as far away from the house as possible. I didn't know what was happening to me. I only knew that it happened whenever I was alone. Despite my fears, I always went back inside the house to check my eyes in the mirror, as after each burning, I had the strange feeling that they had changed colour from dark brown to green, blue, or some lighter colour. Yes, so strong was the force that touched me that it felt as if my eyes had changed colour. I feared the door slamming shut behind me, trapping me inside, but the feeling that whatever had touched me had changed the colour of my eyes was stronger than my fear of being trapped inside. I imagined myself walking on the street to Hya's house and people running away from me, screaming, because of the colour of my eyes.

The burnings had started started a few years earlier, just before my fourteenth birthday, on my first day home, after I was forced to quit school due to financial difficulties. I was lying in bed beside my baby brother, Tom, whom I had just fed. We were about to go to sleep, or so I thought. The next thing I remember is hearing my neighbour, Mr. Albert Prince, who we called Mass Albert, or Dake, calling my name. "Bev! Bev!"

Dake could easily see me lying on the bed from where he was standing by the open door. I heard him calling my name again and again, but I was unable to respond physically. It seemed as if I was hearing his voice from high above, somewhere in the sky. I kept saying, "I'm coming, Dake, I'm coming. Hold on. I'll be with you in a minute."

I got up as soon as I could and called out to Dake. He had by now given up on waking me and had left for his home. He heard me calling him and stopped underneath the cherry tree that bordered our land and his.

"Mass Albert! Mass Albert! Were you calling me?"

He said, "Bev, you're surely a sound sleeper. I called and called, but you didn't answer. I was passing by your house on my way home and just wanted to let you know that I heard Leo died this morning. He was killed by a train somewhere close to Parnassus."

I didn't respond with the shock Dake had expected such tragic news to bring. Leo was a quiet, young man who was liked by everyone in the community. He rented a room at my grandmother Ya Ya's old house, which we commonly referred to as "Over Yard" because it is situated across the street. Leo's untimely death was going to be a great shock to the entire community. The time was now around ten o'clock in the morning. I was among the first to hear the news. Most would find out when they returned home from school or work in the evening. But I couldn't register shock at this sad news, as I was more puzzled about where I was when Dake was calling my name. Dake too was puzzled, but for another reason.

"Bev, you don't seem surprised. Did you hear about this before?"

"No, no, you're the first to tell me. Gosh, I'm really sorry to hear—"

"I'm sorry if I interrupted your sleep, but I just thought you'd like to know."

"It's okay, Dake. It's just that I'm feeling a bit tired. Thank you for telling me."

Dake walked away, still perplexed at my calm response to this tragic news. I was having a hard time trying to imagine Leo being dead, while at the same time, my own crisis occupied most of my mind. I knew I wasn't dreaming.

After that day, the burnings occurred at least twice daily—early in the morning and when I went to bed at night. I learned to recognize the signs—things such as the normal sounds of traffic, people, birds, and dogs suddenly going silent. I'd try to get up off the bed and run out of the house, but my limbs would become paralyzed. The more I struggled, the more exhausted I felt when I came out of it, and the more burned I felt—as though my entire body was on fire.

The more I prayed, the more the burnings increased. The frequency increased to three times daily—early in the morning, again between nine o'clock and noon, and again just before I drifted off to sleep at night. Although I knew the signs, I was still unable to predict with any certainty exactly when it would occur. So I took every precaution to ensure I was never alone. But that was difficult to always achieve. I was just about the only child not attending school, and most of the adults were at work, so I really didn't have anyone to talk to. Moreover, I enjoyed being alone with books. They were my means of escaping the world I was forced to live in. I loved the words, the places, the ideas, and the worlds they transported me to, and I dreamed of the day I'd be old enough to travel.

As the burnings continued, I questioned what was happening to me. At first, I wondered if it was real or if I was suffering from some brain or sleeping disorder. I thought it was a medical problem. I looked up the symptoms in a medical dictionary, searching for some medical term to describe my problem. Epileptic seizures seemed to come closest to what I was experiencing, and I would have even welcomed that unfortunate malady, except for one inescapable fact: my "seizures" only happened when I was alone. It was impossible to have a selective type of epileptic seizure that only occurred when I was alone, lasted for about fifteen minutes each time, and ended whenever someone needed me or was about to arrive. And no one had ever witnessed me having a seizure. If I was having periodic bouts of fainting spells, then someone would see that too. This illness only occurred when I was lying down and alone. I came across no such illness in the medical journal. I had no money to visit the doctor or any proof that it was really happening. I couldn't go around complaining of invisible symptoms and an illness no one else could see.

Next I theorized that my dreadful experiences may be the work of aliens from outer space carrying out experiments on me. I knew aliens were powerful beings with technology far beyond ours, but I didn't think they, or their spaceships, were invisible. Finally, I reasoned that my problem was with an intelligent being—a spirit—who knew exactly when to strike. The cause emanated from outside rather than inside my body. And lurking in the back of my mind was the growing belief that, somehow, I knew the person who was doing it—the name seemed poised on the tip of my tongue. As this feeling grew stronger, a name flashed through my mind and then vanished just as quickly. Out of desperation, I shouted, "I know you! I know who you are. You are a spirit! And you are a man!" And then immediately I questioned, "Are you a man?" I wanted to ask who he was and why he was doing this to me. But no answer came, so I didn't want to ask any more questions. I simply began to refer to him as "The Man."

To exacerbate what was already a confusing state of affairs, there followed a series of events that could be attributed to either good or evil spirits. I had a habit of sleeping with my face pressed against the wall. This was the safest position to offer protection from what or who was bothering me. One night while I was in a deep sleep, from somewhere in my mind I heard a man's gentle voice waking me, saying, "Bev, Bev, move slowly away from the wall." Not only did I hear the voice, but I also felt someone holding me gently, guiding me in the right direction away from the wall, saying, "That's it, slowly, slowly," as I obeyed his prompt. When I was at a safe distance, I opened my eyes to see a huge scorpion with its tail poised, ready to strike me in the eye. I didn't see anyone, but the voice commanded, "Get up and kill the scorpion!"

Under normal circumstances, I would have been so terrified of the scorpion that I would have run and shouted for someone to come and kill it for me. Yet without thinking, I obeyed the voice, grabbed an empty pop bottle, and ground the scorpion to a pulp. I wasn't scared of most insects, but I was terrified of scorpions. Generally whenever I saw one, I became so paralyzed with fear that I couldn't move to kill it. But that night, responding to the commanding voice, I crushed the scorpion with the bottle until I was certain it was very dead.

Immediately afterwards, my old fear of scorpions resurfaced, and I refused to get back into bed. I sat on a chair with my hands and feet firmly tucked to my chest, keeping them well away from the floor in case there were more scorpions around. My clothes brushing against my skin caused me to panic and shake with fear, thinking it was a scorpion. I remained sitting on the chair in that position for a long while, intending to stay there until morning when I would be able to see everything much more clearly.

Then it hit me. The Man told me to do something, and I obeyed without thinking. *Surely,* I thought, *the voice is that spirit. I obeyed the voice of a spirit.* I started praying. "Oh God, please forgive me. I didn't mean to obey the voice of a spirit. Spirits are evil. I want to obey your voice only. Please forgive me." I went back to bed after praying, as the chair was proving a rather uncomfortable place to spend the night.

Other experiences were even more disturbing, but I don't care to go into them here. My experiences, both good and evil, left me confused about the nature of The Man. Sometimes I wondered if he was someone who loved me, died, and wanted to be my guardian angel. Perhaps when the moon was full, or something of the kind, he just went crazy and couldn't help changing into some animal that wanted to hurt me. I thought I might have watched too many strange shows on television, or perhaps one too many scary movies. Whatever the cause, one thing was clear: I needed help, and I needed it urgently. The kind of help I needed could only come from God. Protecting me from the scorpion was a good thing, and surely it wasn't a human being who had woken me to tell me about the impending danger. I began praying to God more fervently, asking Him to take The Man away and let me return to a normal life.

As time passed, I realized that God wasn't answering my prayers, so I made a deal with him. In addition to the prayers forced out of me each morning and before I went to sleep, I began to read the book of Psalms in the Bible. I thought God would answer my prayers when I got to the end. I read through every psalm, but still there was no help. I extended the deadline to reading the entire New Testament. I read from the Bible each morning and night, but still no help, so I extended the mission even further to reading the Bible in its entirety, from Genesis to Revelation.

As I read the Old Testament, I wondered if God's failure to answer my previous requests was added proof that he didn't exist or simply didn't care. The more I read and prayed, the more the burnings seemed to increase. I continued to fight to maintain consciousness. I refused to go under without a fight, and I fought with all my might. I yelled out God's name, calling for his help. My prayers became more desperate, with tears and supplications.

I finished reading the book of Genesis without trouble, but for some reason when I got to Exodus, I lost control when Moses ascended Mt. Sinai, communicated with God, and descended with the Ten Commandments. I began pounding the Bible at this section. I erupted in tears and beseeched God, saying, "God, I need help! You have to help me! You have to help me! You *have* to exist! You *must* exist! The Man is going to kill me one of these days!"

My heart was breaking, but still I prayed, "God, you must exist. You have to exist. If humans made these commandments, they would be much easier. Humans want to commit adultery. They wouldn't say, 'Thou shalt not commit adultery.' They'd say, 'You can have as many women as you like.' They want to break the other commandments when it suits them. Humans wouldn't state the commandments so plainly and concisely. They'd put clauses in them. You have to exist! You have to care! You have to help me now, because I have no more strength to fight. I'm tired of holding on. I'm going to let go. I'm going to stop believing in you."

But I didn't give up. I kept on reading the Bible to fulfill my promise to God, in the hope that he would come through for me. Reading the whole Bible meant the perfection and completion of a journey of faith toward God. Still, the burnings continued. If God wouldn't help me, I thought, then I would have to try to get rid of The Man myself.

I made a cross of twigs and put it under my pillow. I planned to hold it up and repeat the Lord's Prayer and the Shepherd's Psalm whenever I sensed The Man's presence. In short, it was my way of carrying out an exorcism to banish The Man from my life. I don't know why I thought I'd have time to hold up the cross before I became paralyzed, but I was beyond desperate and feeling a growing sense of helplessness. I had to do something to save myself from my invisible enemy.

Also, I believed that if I left the cross lying on my bed or pillow, or beside my Bible on the standing dinner tray that served as my nightstand, The Man would see it and leave me in peace while I was sleeping. So I made my cross and placed it near me at night or whenever I was alone. I kept it hidden from my family and friends because I didn't know how to explain it to them.

The cross didn't work.

Shortly after my Exodus cry, The Man entered the room. Once again, I was paralyzed, and, as usual, I started praying the Lord's Prayer and yelling for God to help me. I heard, or rather sensed, The Man stifling a laugh. I freaked out. "Oh God! Oh my God! This is not your average spirit that's bothering me. Instead of fearing or fleeing from the cross or the Lord's Prayer, he's amused by them. This must be a demon. What am I going to do now? What's going to happen to me? I'm in the hands of a demon, and God is nowhere to be found!"

Just then I heard a voice say, "Bev, how can you fight me with my own words? Don't you know there are two kinds of spirits in the world?"

"God, what are you talking about? The Man was laughing at me, my cross, and my prayers," I cried out, without realizing I had used the word "God" in my response.

As I recovered from this burning, I pondered the words I had heard. The voice had said, "There are two kinds of spirits in the world." If there were two kinds of spirits, was it possible that it was God, as well as the devil, who was responsible for what was happening to me? There was only one way to find out. I decided that the next time the burning started to happen, I was going to say, like Samuel, "*Speak; for thy servant heareth* [is listening]" (1 Samuel 3:10). If God responded when I said this, then there would be no doubt that it was indeed the Lord. And if it was God, then I was going to have to give up any dreams of living life on my terms. I dreamed of going to New York and Hollywood to work while attending school, then to dance Friday and Saturday nights away in the nightclubs. Perhaps, strangely, I was sort of hoping it was the devil, because then God would deliver me and I'd be free to pursue my life as planned. So the next time it happened, I said, "Speak, Lord, thy servant heareth." I waited for a response, but there was only silence.

It was getting difficult to hide what was happening to me from Dolsie. She had noticed me getting upset for no reason and asked what was going on. I told her about The Man and the burnings, and that the burning wasn't the only abnormal thing that was happening to me. I was experiencing moments of déjà vu as well. I'd hear news of someone's death or go to a place I'd never been before and feel that I'd heard or seen it all before. I believed it was evil to have knowledge of this sort, so I'd try to keep it to myself, hoping it would all go away.

As a child, I always had a strong sixth sense. Someone I hadn't seen in a while would pop into my mind, then they'd show up the next day. Or I'd smell someone before I saw or heard them. I remember my mother telling me to stop telling people I knew they were coming because I smelled them, as that wasn't a nice thing to say to someone. The word I was looking for back then was that I sensed they were coming.

I'd also have premonitions of something happening to a family member, like the time when my siblings and I were spending the holidays with my paternal grandmother in Kingston, and I told my siblings I needed to go home because something was happening to our mother. I kept crying that I wanted to go home, until Granny got mad and sent us home. About four hours later, we arrived home in Clarendon only to have my paternal aunt meet us at the bus stop and confirm what I had said to my brother and sister. My brother and sister looked at me then and said, "That's exactly what you said in Kingston." It didn't seem strange to me then, just natural. But the idea of seeing things again—someone told me later it's called déjà vu—bothered me as much as being burned.

When we heard some tragic news or attended a funeral, Dolsie would ask, "Did you 'see' this one before?"

I would reply, "Yes" or "not yet," then explain why.

Usually it took a "key" to trigger my memory. For example, someone might walk into church during the funeral wearing a new dress, and the pattern of that dress would unlock my memory. Sometimes the events happened in the form of a dream that I didn't remember until the key opened the door to recollection.

Feeling frustrated, helpless, and powerless, I cried and belaboured my fate, praying it away. Dolsie often said, "Bev, it could be a gift from God. Maybe you're one of those mother (medium) women who can see things before they happen. I think the reason you can't remember things fully to warn someone they're in danger is because you won't go to church. Maybe if you go to church and start living right, the gift will become more developed."

I brushed her idea off. "I don't think so. It's evil. I want God to take it away."

Still, I couldn't shake the feelings of guilt that perhaps I could have played an important role in either preventing someone from dying or preparing them for some tragic news. I convinced myself that this gift was the work of the devil. I most certainly didn't want to see or know things before they happened. Perhaps I didn't want to see the entire picture. It was easier to believe the devil was out to get me than to believe God was calling me. If God was indeed calling me, I was neither ready nor willing to give my life over to Him. And what was I expected to do with the feeling that I'd been somewhere when I knew for a fact that I'd never been there before? What purpose could that serve? Nothing was clear. My life was like a giant jigsaw puzzle that I couldn't put together because there were missing pieces.

But there was one clue to all that was happening to me—it just didn't register in my brain at the time. After each burning event while I waited on the steps for my body to cool down and my strength to return, I'd get the feeling I used to have when I'd return from Sunday school and church. I couldn't adequately describe the feeling or what it meant, but I'd have it all day on Sundays after I changed out of my church clothes and back into my play clothes. It felt like a warm glow that radiated from the inside and spread all over me with peace and love. It didn't make much sense to me, so I never bothered to explore the feeling.

I believed God would eventually rescue me and I would return to a normal life, pursue my dreams as planned, and no one would ever know that anything supernatural had happened to me.

As mentioned earlier, Dolsie lived down the road from me and usually came to my house around 10:30 a.m. to get me so we could go to her cousin Hya's house to play dominoes or card games on the verandah. I usually lay on the bed reading a book, with the radio on, as I waited for her. I was the only one home, as the others were off to work or school. It turned out that I was getting burned during the time I waited for Dolsie to arrive. Dolsie took one look at my face and asked, "Did it happen again?"

"Yes," I said. "He knows how to time your arrival. He leaves just about the time you turn the corner onto my street. I'm not going to wait here for you anymore. Just go straight to Hya's and I'll be there waiting for you." There was no way I was going to wait there and get burned if I could help it. From the on, I ran off to Hya's house as soon as I was through cleaning the house and washing the dishes.

After hastily completing my household chores one morning, I ran out the door to get to Hya's house. I got as far as the gate when something caused me to look up. I saw a fiery ball about the size of a soccer ball. It was trailing light like a comet and travelling at high speed towards me. It appeared as if it had fallen away from the sun and was hurtling directly toward me. I turned and ran for the safety of my house as fast as I could, crying, "Yes, God! Yes, God! I know it's you. I know it's you." I instinctively threw both hands up over my head for protection, afraid the fiery ball was going to land on me and consume me with fire. Judging its speed, I dove for the steps, fell on my hands and knees, and crawled inside the house to my bedside.

I knelt by my bed and prayed, tears streaming down my face. "Yes, God. Yes, God, I know it's you. I know you've been calling me, but ... but I'm so young. I'm too young. I don't have enough experience to be used by you. I haven't had any fun yet." I told God about my childhood, crying that life had been very unkind to me and that I needed some time to myself to discover who I was. I told him I was tired of being a little mother to my siblings, taking care of everybody, with no time for myself. I pleaded for him to return when I turned thirty years old, and I promised that I'd be ready to serve him then. Thirty seemed like a ripe age to retire from the nightclub scene, hang up my dancing shoes, and serve the Lord. By then I would have gotten all the wanderlust and desire to dance out of my system. But at that point, quickly reconsidering, I prayed, "Please, God, please come back when I'm forty. I'll be more mature and ready to follow you." I cried my heart out until I felt I had persuaded God to see my point of view, then I got up and continued to Hya's house, glancing nervously up at the sun.

As I walked, I thought, *Why are you calling me? Why do you have to call me? Why don't you call Merna? Call Dolsie. Call Yvonne. Why are you calling me? Is it because I'm such a goody-two-shoes? I regret being such a goody-two-shoes. I wish I was more like Yvonne—then you wouldn't be calling me.*

Although I first confided in Dolsie, I later, to a lesser extent, told my other girlfriends—Elaine, better known as Blackie, and Winsome, Hya's sister—about the déjà vu stuff. But I said nothing about the burnings. I was reluctant to mention those experiences to anyone for fear of being called crazy. For the longest time, I kept everything to myself, unable to offer proof of what was happening to me.

Around noon on a day I was expecting Blackie to visit, I was alone and lying on the bed at a friend's house in May Pen, waiting for her to arrive. I heard her steps coming up the gravel path and her voice calling me, but I couldn't respond, as I was experiencing another burning. Blackie walked into the house, took one look at me on the bed, and ran out screaming, "Lord, Lord, Bev is dying! Bev is dying!"

I regained my senses and ran after her, somewhat tired but also very relieved. After assuring Blackie that I was okay, I asked, "What did you see?"

"I saw your eyes rolling up in your head with only the whites showing, and you were just lying there looking as if you were dying."

I assured her again that I was fine and that I was probably just dreaming. But deep down I knew that was the last stage of my resisting becoming unconscious after being zapped. That day—three, almost four, years after the first burning—was the first proof I ever had that what was happening to me was real, not just something in my mind. Blackie, without knowing it, had confirmed the final moments of what happened each time I experienced a burning.

For a month or two in my late teens, I returned to church after having left around age thirteen. I was struggling with staying or leaving. While at Hya's house one day, Hya looked at me thoughtfully and said, "Bev, stay in church. God is calling you."

Curious, I asked, "What makes you say that? How do you know God is calling me?"

"I can't put my finger on it, but it's written all over your face." Hya was one of my dancing and movie buddies. She didn't attend church, yet she could plainly see that I was hiding something from her.

I simply smiled and said, "I know."

By then, I was a four-year veteran of the burnings but still uncertain about the cause. Perhaps I didn't truly want to know. I didn't even consider the possibility that it might've been God. Sometimes I thought it was God, and other times I was convinced it wasn't. After all, there was the voice and the calm presence that had saved me from the scorpion, but on several occasions, evil was definitely at work.

If I didn't try to fight or resist, the burning didn't hurt. But my fight-or-flight instinct would take over. Once the atmosphere went quiet, I could neither fight nor take flight. All I could do was fight by keeping my eyes open for a minute or so. I called out for God and those around, but no one ever heard me. I fought so hard. Once I managed to escape when a sympathetic voice said, "Aw, let's let her go this time."

Let's let her go? Are there others working together with The Man? Are aliens from outer space carrying out terrible experiments on me? I wondered.

I had somehow come to terms with this aspect of my life. There was absolutely nothing I could do about it. Most weekday mornings, I'd lie in bed listening to *The Good Morning Man Show,* hosted by one of my favourite radio deejays, Alan Magnus, as my sister got ready to leave for school. The burnings became part of this routine. I felt myself slipping into unconsciousness, saying in my mind, *Goodbye, Alan Magnus, I'll be back in about fifteen minutes.* And I'd be back after having missed part of the radio show.

Oddly, my time spent unconscious was mostly blank. I could recall only a few bits and pieces of events that took place when I returned to consciousness. One such memory was of me going swiftly across the sky via a narrow, rusted tunnel—like a pipeline made from iron or steel. A man was holding my hand, and we were going through this tunnel at a rapid speed. My head was very close to the top of the tunnel, and I kept yelling, "I'm going to bump my head. I'm going to bump my head!" But we kept going until I emerged safely from the tunnel without bumping my head. But I don't know what happened after that.

These experiences made no sense, but they were the bits and pieces I remembered upon regaining consciousness. I was in a continual state of questioning, wondering whether what was happening was no more than a sleep disorder I had exaggerated and made into something it wasn't. Could the answer be that my body fell asleep while I was still awake? It simply made no sense that God could be involved. It made more sense that the devil was slowly killing me, tormenting me to prove that God didn't care about me one bit.

CHAPTER TWO

What Shall I Write?

About a year after my encounter with Jesus, I immigrated to Canada to live with my Aunt Callie. She was the one who had taken me and all the children in the family to church with her when we were too young to attend by ourselves. I'd been asking to come and live with her ever since I'd quit school, and she'd finally said yes. Several days after my arrival, I began feeling that something was missing from my life. After a while, it dawned on me that The Man and the burnings were gone. I started laughing. Yes, I was finally free of The Man. He was back in Jamaica. I imagined him showing up the day I left and the day after, looking for me. I laughed even more as I tried to picture the look on his face when he failed to find me at my home or the places where I stayed in Jamaica. I went to bed happy that night, feeling free and happy to be a normal human being again.

I laughed too soon. About a week after I arrived in my new country, I woke up in the morning with a sad, dreadful feeling. *Oh no, The Man is back!* He had found me. He hadn't really lost track of me. He was simply giving me time to become acquainted with my new environment, or even to miss him. My life in Canada, where I thought I'd escaped The Man, resumed with the usual dose of burnings, prayers to God to be rid of The Man, Bible reading, and partying.

Then, in the second year of my new life in Canada, what I feared the most happened. It was around nine or ten o'clock in the morning on a bright, cold spring day. I was home alone, in a new house, miles from where I used to live. Feeling sleepy, I decided to lie down in the living room, where the sun shone brightly through the windows, to get some rest before cleaning the house. I pulled the curtains back to allow the sunshine to brighten the room and make it less scary to be alone. I lay on the carpet in front of the television, intending to relax or sleep for a while. It wasn't long before I began to feel the familiar sense of paralysis take control of my limbs. I put up the usual fight and prayer. I fought so hard that I won. I got up and made a run for the door, but when I reached the door, I stopped suddenly in my tracks. "What the heck's going on here?" I asked myself out loud. "Whose body did I just jump over?"

I was the only one in the house. I'd taken the children to school and the adults were at work. I turned back to see who it was. To my horror, the person was wearing the same green army pants and green, white, and blue sleeveless top I was wearing. And she was lying in the same place and position I'd just abandoned. I moved closer, hesitantly, and saw myself, face to face, for the first time without the aid of a mirror. I began to weep. "Oh my God, I'm dead. I'm dead! You killed me! You finally did it! I knew this would happen one day. You and your darned experiments! You keep taking me out of my body and putting me back in. Now something's gone wrong, and you can't put me back in."

I imagined the news of my death reaching my family and friends. "They're going to be so sad when they hear that I died," I cried. "They won't even know that death doesn't hurt." Dolsie popped into my mind. I thought about how much she was going to miss me and about the times we'd spent together going to the movies and nightclubs, having fun chatting and laughing with the guys and our circle of friends. She would probably recall how she'd told me to go to church and let God into my life and how I had refused. "I'm going to miss them." I cried even harder. "I'm not ready to leave them yet." I sat down beside myself, cradling my head in my lap, looking at my face and moaning, "Poor mi Bev. Poor mi Bev" (the Jamaican form of "My poor Bev").

Then I raised my head and screamed, "I want to go back into my body! I want to go back into my body!" My screams tore through the house. I saw a human form over me and sensed the presence of The Man in the room. He was standing in the air above me, but there was little else for me to identify him.

Immediately I popped back into my body, and my heart began beating. The sound of my heartbeat was so loud I could hear it, but it was sweet music to my ears. I felt the blood rushing through my body like a tap turned on to the maximum. My legs felt like lead, and my whole body was too weak to move. I remained lying down like that for a while and got up as soon as I was able to. Still very weak, I struggled toward the front door to run outside but didn't quite make it. My legs gave way, and I collapsed and passed out in the hallway. I remember it clearly, because to this day, that was the only time in my life that I fainted.

I regained consciousness, sat up slowly, and shakily got to my feet. Then I stumbled out the door to sit on the steps in the morning sun, glad to be back in my body and at the same time trying to come to terms with what had just taken place. Some thirty minutes to an hour later, I realized that I was only dressed in a thin, sleeveless top, and my feet were bare. I was in such a state of shock that I didn't feel the cold. I dreaded going back into the house, but I had no choice. I wasn't dressed for spring, so I couldn't take a walk to the nearby mall or around the block.

In the evening, the family returned from work and school. They asked, "And how was your day, Bev?"

I replied, "It was okay." But deep down I was thinking, *If I told you the truth, would you believe me?*

My near-death experience didn't change my focus one bit. I didn't know what to make of it, yet I didn't run to church or draw closer to God. Instead, I continued to hang out at These Eyes, a nightclub I assumed was named after the popular song, "*These Eyes*" by The Guess Who. *These Eyes*, on Pape at Cosburn, not far from the Pape subway, was a social hub for many Black and Caribbean youth in the Greater Toronto Area. Its slogan was "These Eyes, the place to socialize." And boy, did we ever socialize.

I also spent some Friday and Saturday nights at Mama G's with other young people from every racial, cultural, religious, and socio-economic background. Mama G's was in the heart of Toronto, in the Yonge and Dundas area. Here, Catholics, Jews, and Protestants danced, chatted, ate, drank, and laughed together without a care in the world. That was the life I wanted—not a care in the world.

One night at Mama G's, I heard a clear voice above the loud music say, "Bev, you don't belong here. This is not what I brought you to Canada for." I felt guilty, out of place, and lonely, but I wanted so desperately to fit in with the party crowd and have fun. Try as I did, I just couldn't rid myself of the voice. But I didn't leave. I just sat silently with my friends, with my arms folded across my chest.

"Bev, are you okay? You're so quiet tonight. Are you cold?" asked my friends.

They were all looking at me, concerned.

"I'm all right," I said, unconvincingly.

"Would you like to dance?" asked another.

I got up to dance, to try to shake the feelings away, but I couldn't get into the groove. I returned to my seat and sat thinking that after such a hard life, I deserved some enjoyment, but God wouldn't let me. Finally, I couldn't stand it any longer and stomped off to the washroom to have a talk with God.

"God," I said, "what am I doing here that's wrong? What's wrong with dancing and having fun? I'm not doing anything wrong. I'm not hurting anyone. I work hard all week. I've had a tough life. Surely I deserve to relax and have some fun on weekends." With that off my chest, I marched back out to have some fun.

Around that time, I was also struggling to reconcile the God of the Old and the New Testaments. My issue was that I saw people in and around Toronto who looked like the Jesus I encountered in Jamaica—namely the Jewish people. I even lived, worked, and went dancing with some of them. I learned not to mention the name of Jesus in their presence, because they didn't believe in him. How could the whole Bible be taken seriously if the people of the Old Testament didn't believe in the New Testament? How could this be? It was too confusing for me. In confusion, I said, "I wash my hands clean of the whole thing."

I was angry with God for causing all the uncertainty about who Jesus is. I told God I didn't want anything to do with the Bible, because he couldn't get things straight. *If Jesus is of you, then why or how could you allow his own people to deny him to this day, while much of the rest of the world embraces him?* Even though I was running from God, I knew Jesus was real. But where did I, from the sugar cane belt of rural Jamaica, or my knowledge stand with devout Jews? I saw them walking to the synagogue early in the morning and on the Sabbath. They looked so wise, so knowledgeable, so committed in their holy attire, and I feared I couldn't attain to such a high standard of knowledge, dedication, and holiness.

Still, I believed I had the right to be angry with God and, in rebellion, to live as I pleased. When asked what my religion was, I'd respond rather abruptly, "I'm not religious." After responding like that one day, a still, small voice inside of me said, "That's right, you are not religious. You seek God and the truth, not religion."

I was also at that time searching for something to do as a career. I was planning to go back to school and then to university, but I had no idea what I wanted to pursue. I was in my early twenties and still not sure what I wanted to do with my life. I worked to pay the bills and buy nice clothes, but it was temporary. I wanted to do something more satisfying with my life. But what?

Talking with a friend one day, I bemoaned the fact that most people knew from a young age what they wanted to be when they grew up. At that age, I still had no clue. "I don't even know why I was born," I complained. "I can't seem to find my niche in life." The gist of the conversation was that I wasn't happy with my job and wanted to do something better in life. Suddenly, an open book appeared in front of me, but my friend couldn't see the book. The words on the pages were written in English, yet I couldn't decipher them. I peered intensely on the two pages in front of me, trying to read them, but try as I might, I just couldn't make out any of the words. Then, just as quickly as it appeared, the book was gone.

Not long after that conversation, I got up for work and took my usual fifteen-minute walk to Chester subway. From there, I took a westbound train to the Yonge and Bloor station and then boarded the northbound train to Lawrence East station, followed by a fifteen-minute bus ride to work. I got off at my stop and took my usual shortcut through a clearing surrounded by trees to the west and houses and buildings nearby. As I walked, I questioned my purpose in life and felt downcast, because I should have been going to university, not doing this job. Then what seemed to be the sun suddenly went dark, and a moment later it reappeared. It was as if it had blinked or someone had flipped a light switch off and on in a dark room.

I looked up at the sun, and it was peering back at me as innocently and indifferently as ever. *Perhaps it was my imagination. No, it was not.* Something strange had just happened. If it wasn't the sun, then it was me. Maybe I was having a heart attack. I grabbed the left side of my chest. "Oh God, I'm having a heart attack!" I cried. I was in my early twenties, five-feet-six, one-hundred-and-sixteen pounds, and in good health, but I had no other explanation for what had made the sun appear to behave in such a strange manner. As I stood there wondering, the sun began to descend toward the Earth at a rapid speed. Underneath the sun was a shining angel, descending. He was dressed in a long, shimmering, white gown and holding a glistening sword in one hand. I stood there for a few seconds, fascinated by my first sighting of an angelic being.

Ever since I was a little girl, I wondered why when angels appeared to people in the Bible, the people were always afraid. Their fear always forced the angels to say, "Fear not" or "Be not afraid." I told myself that angels are my people, my Bible people. If and when one appeared to me, I was going to giggle and laugh with delight, because I knew they wouldn't do me any harm. Angels were my friends. They would never need to say "Fear not" to me. The angel got closer, and as he got closer, I realized it was Jesus! With a sword in his hand! Immediately, a passage from the Bible popped into my mind: "*Then I looked, and behold, a white cloud, and on the cloud sat One like the Son of Man, having on His head a golden crown, and in His hand a sharp sickle*" (Revelation 14:14, NKJV).

There was no time to draw comparisons between a sickle and a sword or between symbolic and literal. "Oh my God! Oh my God! The world is ending today, and I'm not ready to meet God." I turned away from Jesus, looking for a place to hide. I started running toward a house with its garage door open.

Halfway to the garage, I turned around to see how fast Jesus was gaining on me. But Jesus was no longer moving toward me. He was standing in the air, close to the trees, but now he was holding the sword behind him with both hands, one on either end. I stopped running and walked back to him. I wasn't afraid of Jesus. I wanted to be near him. I wanted to look at him and talk to him, but I was afraid of the sword and judgement. Still wary of the sword, I drew closer. Without opening his mouth, I heard Jesus say, "Go back to church."

I said, "Yes, Lord. Yes, Lord. I'm going back to church. I'm going back to church."

He paused for a moment, then added, "There is work for you to do."

I breathed a big sigh of relief. He hadn't come to punish me. The world was not ending today. As I stood there looking at Jesus, I noticed that He was larger than any human. He was at least twenty feet tall, and had a golden cord tied around his chest instead of his waist, and there was shiny stuff all around him, which reminded me of fireworks at Ontario Place. Jesus stood there for a while as I continued to look, and then he simply vanished right in front of my eyes.

That encounter happened around ten o'clock in the morning. After Jesus's appearance, I walked the remaining distance to my workplace. I got to work with all kinds of feelings and thoughts racing through my mind. That was a close call indeed. My morning experience stayed with me all day. I couldn't tell it to anyone at work, because they were Jewish. It would have to wait until I got home. I didn't know what kind of work I could do in the church, and I didn't ask. I was just grateful for a second chance at life. I couldn't sing, and I had a major fear of speaking in front of an audience, so I couldn't preach or teach either.

On the way home from work, I had an overwhelming urge to stop at the store and buy writing paper. After my purchase, I hurried home and began writing anything and everything that came to mind—mostly poems, but nothing about God or church.

I shared the events of that morning with my roommate, Christine, when she got home from work. I mentioned to her also, and eventually to others, that this was the second time I'd seen Jesus. They warned, "Bev, you have to go to church and stay in church. Don't let him have to come back a third time. You may not be so lucky next time."

I found that it was easier to promise to go back to church than to actually go back to church. I didn't really mind going to church on Sundays, but I wanted to go dancing on the weekends as well. But keeping my promise to Jesus—and the shiny sword—in mind, I called Sharon M., one of my dancing friends, who was from my community in Jamaica and who, like me, used to attend church in Jamaica. She had expressed a desire to return to church but, like me, was finding it difficult to give up going to the nightclubs and parties on weekends.

"Remember our talk about going back to church?" I asked.

"Yeah."

"Let's start going back to church this Sunday." We didn't have a specific church in mind, since we were both relatively new to Canada.

"Which one?"

"I'm not sure, but there are a few churches on St. Clair Avenue. We can start our search there."

I chose to go to St. Clair Avenue West, because someone had invited and taken me to a church there once, and I had noticed quite a few familiar church names from back home on that street. I looked through my closet to find the only dress that didn't have a cut in the back, front, or side to expose a part of my body.

I got dressed on Sunday and met Sharon at St. Clair West subway station to go in search of a church. We took the train, then got on a streetcar with the intent to peer out the window until we found a church. Then we'd get off and walk in. On the streetcar, we saw someone dressed in her Sunday best, and we asked her if we could go with her to her church. She was more than happy to have us accompany her.

On the way home, Sharon looked at me with astonishment and asked, "What's happened to your face?"

"Oh, you mean the pimples and stuff? I get them all the time, and no matter what I use, they just won't go away."

"No, no, there's something different about your face. It didn't look like that this morning," she explained, still staring at my face. My face was literally glowing, and Sharon kept staring at it in amazement all the way home. That glow happened each time I visited a church. Prior to that, I would visit a church, go home, and friends and neighbours would say, "Something's different about you. You're glowing. What happened to you today?"

"Oh," I'd reply, smiling, "I went to church and an angel kissed me."

Sharon and I both made up our minds to continue going to church on Sundays, and we did for a while, but the weekend dancing gradually began to win out again. It was a real struggle between our two desires, and after a couple of Sundays, Sharon didn't feel like going to church anymore. Going to church alone while my friends were out having fun on weekends left me feeling resentful and angry. I was angry about being singled out by God to attend church when I really didn't want to. *Why me? Why did God have to call me when he had so many faithful people in church just dying for him to call on them?*

My other party friends asked, "Why are you going to church? How come you gave up all the nice clothes and partying? Why are you wasting your youth? Why are you throwing your life away in church? Some guy must've done broke your heart." I couldn't, and I wouldn't, tell them the truth, so I kept going to church, even though I wasn't thrilled about what I had to give up.

In truth, I wasn't fully committed to attending church right away after my second visit from Jesus. I was looking around for a church to become a member of, but in the meantime, I was bargaining with God to let me continue to have fun in the nightclubs. I loved dancing to the latest songs, learning the new dance moves, as well as grooving to the oldies. I searched for them on the radio, turned the volume up, and danced up a storm all by myself, just like I used to do back home in Jamaica with Dolsie, Yvonne, Winsome, and Hya.

Knowing the latest dance moves and the lyrics of the hottest songs was high on my priority list. I loved to predict which one would make it to the top of the charts. I laughed for joy whenever my predictions came true. As the song grew more popular, I found myself pleading with God, "Please, God, please, just this last one. Please let me go to the nightclubs and dance to this one, and I'll commit to going to church right after this song." I heard myself pleading, again, "Please, God, after this one." I meant it, but the hits just kept coming, and I kept pleading.

Weekends were the hardest. On Friday, Saturday, and Sunday nights, I watched the clock, crying like a drug addict whose drug of choice was dancing. Oh, the agony as I watched the clock counting down until I knew the clubs or parties were in full swing. When the hands on the clock hit midnight, I cried even harder, imagining my friends and other clubbers having the time of their lives dancing, chatting, laughing, and meeting new people in the nightclubs and at house parties.

After attending church for some time, I prayed, "God, I don't see anything wrong with dancing, and I can't seem to stop myself from dancing and going to nightclubs. If you want me to quit, you're going to have to take the urge away from me, because I can't help myself." I said this to ease my conscience more than out of any sincere desire to stop. I'd asked God for so many things in the past, and since I hadn't received any help from him, at least not right away, I figured this prayer request would go into the pile of unanswered prayers, leaving me with the excuse of saying I asked God for help and he didn't respond.

To my surprise, right after praying this prayer and asking God to take away the urge, I heard the songs on the radio and didn't feel the desire to get up and dance. I forced myself to go to the nightclubs, but even there I didn't feel like dancing. In fact, I had to force myself onto the dance floor, and even then, each move became a struggle, as if someone or something was holding my legs in a very tight grip. Gradually, I gave up the nightclubs and the clothes that went with that lifestyle. Later, I tearfully parted with my collection of popular music albums.

When we'd first started going back to church, Sharon and I concluded that if we were going to stay in church, we would have to receive the baptism of the Holy Spirit. Both of us had become members of our respective churches back in Jamaica, me for a month or two, and Sharon for a bit longer. But neither church was big on the baptism of the Holy Spirit. Yet we knew that although we had the desire to serve God, we didn't have the strength on our own to resist the temptation to go dancing. Only God, through his Holy Spirit, could help us.

"I think the reason we can't quit the nightclubs and parties and fully commit to serving God is because we've been trying to do so on our own. We need the baptism of the Holy Spirit to help us," Sharon said. And I agreed.

With this revelation in mind, we went to the altar of the church on St. Clair Avenue in Toronto, prayed, and waited for the baptism—Sunday after Sunday for a month or two. While praying for the baptism one Sunday, I felt a powerful jolt of electricity surge through my body, shocking me all over. I looked over at Sharon and smiled. She smiled back at me. She and everyone around us could see that I had finally received the baptism of the Holy Spirit.

Upon receiving the baptism of the Holy Spirit, I realized that the burnings, Sweet Breeze, and the Holy Spirit were the same. I was elated that I'd had the Holy Spirit with me all along. I then understood that God was merely waiting for this invitation from me in order to make himself fully known. After receiving the baptism of the Holy Spirit, the burnings steadily decreased to the point where they became almost non-existent. At first I enjoyed my newfound freedom from the burnings, but after almost ten years of it being a regular part of my day, I actually began to miss it.

I returned home from church that Sunday with this new feeling, this new confidence that it was God who was at work within me, despite my running away from him. The burnings were a result of my behaviour and attitude in resisting and expending all my energy fighting God. Still, I wanted more confirmation or reassurance that it was indeed God. That Sunday evening after church, I lay on the living room sofa and said, "God, if it's really your Spirit causing the burnings and periods of unconsciousness, please do it to me now." Suddenly, I felt the familiar, unearthly quietness as the world went still and my body became numb. At that point, I got scared and said, "God, can I go get my Bible before you proceed further? I'll feel much safer with it." The numbness stopped, and I got up and ran to my bedroom and got my Bible. I returned to the living room and lay on the couch. Placing the Bible on my chest, I said, "I'm ready now."

The numbness began again. I was paralyzed, and the next thing I knew, I was outside and above the apartment building, going up, up, up. The Earth looked like a marble below me. The sun, which had been a bright yellow, began to fade toward sunset as I rose ever higher, until I could no longer see it. As I rose, I noticed a vine-like plant beside me, reaching all the way up from the Earth to the skies and beyond. Its leaves were the colours of the sun. The plant started out green on Earth, then changed to yellow and then to orange as it got higher, as if it was imitating the colours of the sun. When the sun was no longer visible to me, I heard a voice say, "Bev, how do you like my world?"

I looked around in amazement. "God, it's so quiet. It's so peaceful up here. Your world is beautiful, God."

I was in deep, dark space, watching seven to twelve stars dancing in a circle like a clock, each star representing a number or hour. I didn't have the presence of mind to count them, so that's just an estimate. They were so beautiful. I was so taken in by their beauty that it didn't occur to me to count them. I was caught up in the moment, watching the beautiful performance. I felt as though they were dancing just for me. As they danced, they all shimmered, then the first star moved to the second's spot, and the second moved to the third's, and so on. It would probably be easier to draw or animate this than to explain it.

When the stars finished their dance, someone handed me a little girl in a red and white dress with bare feet. I believed it was God, because I was keenly conscious of his presence, yet I could only see his hands. I hugged and kissed the baby, who was about a year old, as if I knew her. I knew this baby was from the future, but it was as though I'd known her all along. She didn't need an introduction. I was still hugging and kissing her when I heard a familiar ring from far, far away. It took a little while to recognize that it was the telephone ringing. The little girl and the scene of dancing stars vanished, and I was back in the living room.

I ran to the kitchen to answer the phone. It was Sharon M. on the other end.

"Bev, I was dialling your number for some time but kept getting a wrong number. I know I dialled the right phone number, but a man kept picking up the phone and saying I had the wrong number. Why are you breathing so hard?"

"I ran to get to the phone."

After I finished speaking to Sharon, my roommate, Rose, woke up and said, "Bev, I passed by when you were sleeping on the sofa. You had the most blissful look on your face. I got jealous and decided to take a nap myself." I simply smiled. I knew I dared not tell her the truth. She wouldn't understand how accurate her description was. It was blissful indeed.

My experiences—frightful, terrifying, confusing, and ultimately joyous and wonderful—brought me along the road to the Truth. All the pieces of my life were coming together to reveal a most beautiful picture. The Holy Spirit was the glue that connected all the pieces.

"*But when the Father sends the Advocate as my representative—that is, the Holy Spirit—he will teach you everything and will remind you of everything I have told you.*" (John 14:26; see also 16:13, NLT). Bit by bit, pieces of memory started coming back to me and began to knit together. The puzzle that was my life began to make sense to me. Knowing for sure that God was involved in the burnings, or the "*fire shut up in my bones*" (Jeremiah 20:9), as Jeremiah so aptly described *his* burnings, answered many questions but also raised a few more.

I used to say that if I ever truly had God's attention, I would ask him a whole lot of questions about why my life and the world in general were so messed up. Yet when I stood in his presence, I could only savour the peace and beauty of his world. I asked myself why, of all the questions God could've asked me, did he ask how I liked his world? Then I recalled myself as a little girl constantly complaining, sometimes stomping my feet and yelling, "God, I hate this stinking world."

A smile spread across my face as I remembered sitting on the verandah at Top Yard one night, literally crying, "God, I hate this stinking world. I don't care if I sound like a weakling, but I've just about had enough with the people down here. The adults are always yelling at me, and the children call me all kinds of names because I'm so skinny."

I looked up to heaven with tears running down my face. My tears seemed to cause a moonbeam to connect to me. I held on to the moonbeam for as long as I could, saying, "God, I know it's hard for you to spot me in this crowd of people on Earth, so please follow this moonbeam and find me, because I don't like it here. I don't like this world."

I was thinking that just as the Jamaica Public Service company went around changing the light bulbs on the streetlights, God must also, from time to time, check on the moon to see if its bulb has gone out and needs to be replaced with a new one. I hoped with all my heart that he was checking on the moon that night. "See my moonbeam and follow it to me," I prayed. That's why I used the tears in my eyes to hold on to the moonbeam for as long as I could, asking God to please, please, follow the moonbeam and come help me.

From the day I'd seen Jesus dressed in shiny white with the golden cord around his chest, it troubled me that the cord wasn't tied around his waist like it was supposed to be. That was the usual place to wear such an accessory. Day and night for months I pondered the significance of that detail. Did it mean that time was short? Without knowing why, it bothered me to no end. I couldn't find any rest in my soul. I felt some-how responsible for the cord moving from the waist to his chest area. I had never before seen anyone wear a belt, sash, or cord tied around their chest.

I prayed, asking God to explain. I wanted to know what I needed to do so that Jesus could wear his cord around his waist and I could be at peace regarding this issue. Immediately, a portion of scripture from the book of Revelation surfaced in my mind. The scripture spoke of Jesus clothed with a golden sash or something about his paps. I got my Bible and sat down to search for the scripture verse. Without turning a page, I opened it directly at Revelation 1. I sat in amazement, staring at the very chapter and verse I was getting ready to search for: *And in the midst of the seven candlesticks one like unto the Son of man, clothed with a garment down to the foot, and girt about the paps with a golden girdle* (Revelation 1:13). I wasn't sure what the word "paps" meant. I assumed it meant navel, because belts and sashes were usually tied about the waist. Something inside directed me to look up the word, so I checked the concordance at the back of the Bible and was equally amazed to discover that it meant breast.

Each time I recalled the visits from Jesus, I described the light above Him as the sun. I was in the process of doing so once again when a voice asked, "Bev, the sun?"

"Yes," I replied. "It's the sun that I saw."

"What would happen to the Earth if the sun came that close to it?" the voice asked.

"It would be destroyed," I said, suddenly realizing the error in my argument. "But, but," I stammered, trying to reconcile what I'd seen with scientific fact, "the light I saw was as bright as the sun. No light on Earth is so bright, except the sun."

Right then I remembered the story of Jesus's ascension into Heaven. The New Testament states that a cloud received Jesus out of the disciples' sight (Acts 1:9). The light I had seen both times was indeed shaped like a huge cloud. "But clouds have no light of their own," I protested. "The light I saw above Jesus was shaped like a cloud, but clouds don't have rays or beams, and they're definitely not a source of light!"

My Sunday school lessons and my extensive Bible reading during the time of the burnings came into focus. I recalled the pillar of cloud by day and the pillar of fire by night that the Old Testament said followed Moses and the children of Israel in the wilderness (Exodus 13:21). I combined the light I'd seen both times above Jesus with stories of the ascension and the pillar of fire that accompanied Moses, and I never again referred to the light as the sun. I saw Jesus ascending and descending in a light cloud with a big, bright beam—the pillar of light.

One Saturday about two weeks after receiving the baptism of the Holy Spirit, I had a strong desire to go to the library to get some books to read, so I went to the nearby Pape Public Library. I was an avid reader, and like any young woman my age, I enjoyed romance novels. Yet as soon as I walked through the library doors, I was drawn like a magnet to the section marked "Religious." As I looked at the Bible, I thought of how sad it was that the Word of God was in a section called "Religious" when it should've been in a section called "Truth."

As I searched through the books, my eyes landed on one titled *The Dead Sea Scrolls*. "I'm not touching or reading any sea scrolls of the dead,"

I said to myself. *It's probably some Egyptian book of mummies and curses*, I thought as I walked past it. But try as I might, I couldn't resist going back and pulling it out. I looked it over, reading the back cover to find out what it was about, and as I did, a smile gradually spread across my face. "Why, this is more Bible … more Bible stories," I said softly.

As a child, whenever I heard and read Bible stories, they made me hungry for more, but there was no more outside of the Bible. That Saturday in Pape Library, holding *The Dead Sea Scrolls* in my hand, I realized I could read about what happened in Israel before, during, and after the New Testament times. Fascinated by my discovery, I also picked up *The Shroud of Turin*, along with other books on various religions.

The Dead Sea Scrolls satisfied a long hunger, filled a huge scriptural void, and inspired me to find books on archaeology and religions in the Middle East and around the world. When I was through with that book, I devoured books on other religions to find out about their respective beliefs. I didn't want to read books on religions, because I wasn't interested in religion. I was a seeker of truth, and the truth had found me. But the still, small voice said, "Read them for general knowledge." So I read through all the books on the various religions of the world.

I then turned my attention to Jesus. I read the thoughts of those who were for, against, and somewhere between the two ends of the spectrum regarding who Jesus was. I found *The Shroud of Turin* most disturbing, as it forced me to go beyond the beliefs and teachings of my childhood days in Sunday school and ask myself many questions about Jesus: What if Jesus wasn't of God? What if he appeared to me but he wasn't of God? What if …? While reading about the shroud, I became afraid of who Jesus could be without God. That book and others in the "Religious" section raised many questions for me about who Jesus really is. The authors had many credentials and titles before and after their names, and they wrote very eloquently. They were giants in my eyes.

I went back through the Bible to see what Jesus said about himself and God. I researched what Isaiah, the other prophets, and even the Essenes in *The Dead Sea Scrolls* said about the promised messiah. Then I went to God to hear what he had to say about Jesus.

"God, how can I truly know that Jesus is of You? The Jews still don't believe to this day."

I heard a voice clearly say, "Go read their books (books written about and by Jewish people) and see if you find anything that I have said to them that is contrary to what's in the Bible or to what I've shown you." So I began another level of research, covering the last two thousand years of Jewish history, which extended to exploring the history of the world from its earliest stages to the present day. As my knowledge of Jewish history grew, so did my belief in God and Jesus, because I couldn't find anything that God had said to them before, during, or after Jesus that contradicted the New Testament or what he revealed about Jesus.

As I found it easier to write what I wanted to say, I often wrote my prayers to God instead of praying out loud. Ever since I'd lived in Jamaica, whenever I tried to talk or pray, words didn't come easily. One afternoon at home in the apartment I shared with Rose, I began writing a prayer, asking God what he wanted me to do: "Jesus said there's work for me to do. So what is it that you want me to do?"

A voice like thunder roared, "Write!" The voice was so loud, it felt like it could shake the entire high-rise apartment building. In fear, I ran out of the living room, down the hall to my bedroom, and slammed the door shut, trying to hide from the sound of the thunderous voice. I stood in the bedroom, shaking. Then I calmed myself down by saying, "Bev, it's God. Why are you afraid? God isn't going to hurt you." With that, I returned to the living room, somewhat ashamed of my initial reaction.

"God," I said, "I can't write. I don't have anything to write about."

"Can you spell? Can you hold a pen?"

I smiled as memories of my school days in Jamaica flooded my mind. Writing was one of the things I was good at—my teachers in Jamaica told me that many times. They also said I should become a writer. I said to God, "Yes, I can hold a pen and I can spell, but I still don't have anything to write about. What shall I write?"

"Write—and use the Bible as your reference."

So I began writing about my encounters with Jesus. I completed the first two chapters of this book: "The Day Jesus Came out of the Bible" and

"What Shall I Write?" I figured that was what God wanted me to write about. I had no working title for the book. And with the first two chapters finished, I had nothing else to write about. I sat wondering where I should go from there with my writing. A voice said to me, "What did you say your name was again?" Strange question indeed. I thought for a while and then I saw Bev, the Spirit Fighter, coming down the dusty road like a tumbleweed. I started laughing uncontrollably at her and with her.

"Oh my God! Oh my God!" I laughed even louder, eventually shouting in joy, "The Spirit Fighter! The Spirit Fighter! Oh my God! Oh my God! She got her Bible story! She got her Bible story!" I was so elated at the knowledge that God knew me, even way back then, that I just kept laughing uncontrollably. He remembered what I had forgotten.

The voice broke through my laughter. "And are you an author now?"

I thought this a strange question, so I sat puzzled until my mind flashed back to the day at York Town Primary School when Sweet Breeze called me, "Author, Author," and I angrily replied that my name wasn't Arthur. I burst into hysterical laughter at the silly girl I had been and because I was filled with almost uncontrollable exaltation. With the first two chapters completed, I replied, "My name is Bev, the Spirit Fighter, and yes, yes, I am an author now." Still laughing, I picked up the pen and began writing the next three chapters: "The Spirit Fighter," "I Want to Write," and "Author! Author!"

CHAPTER THREE

The Spirit Fighter

The Sprit Fighter came to life one morning when Dake, on his way home, stopped by to complain to my mother about someone who had just cheated him out of some money.

I saw Dake walking up the narrow street to my house, talking loudly to himself. When he came up the lane, he usually took a shortcut to his place through our yard. But today Dake was very upset.

"Man to man is so unjust," he mumbled. "You don't know who to trust."

Dake often stopped to play with my siblings and me when he passed by. We looked forward to this because he would throw us in the air and catch us and play the usual games adults play with little kids, such as peekaboo.

Dake was a kind, gentle, good-natured man who had been best friends with my mother's father, Tom. We sometimes referred to him as Old Tom to differentiate between him and my younger brother, his namesake. Old Tom had died when my mother was about twelve. After that, Dake had assumed the role of father and grandfather to us—first because he was genuinely a good person, but also out of respect for his friend.

As he walked into our yard, my mother asked, "What's wrong, Mass Albert?"

I listened as Dake explained the situation. I was not yet in kindergarten—or basic school, as it's called in Jamaica. As a sugarcane farmer,

Dake owned a dray cart and some mules, which he used to haul his and other people's sugarcane to the Yarmouth sugarcane factory to be processed. I gathered that there had been some kind of disagreement over how much a particular job was worth or how many loads Dake had taken to the factory. Dake was very upset that he hadn't been paid the full amount due.

At the end of his complaint, Dake stated, "I'm leaving this up to Massa God. Massa God is not sleeping." With that, he walked on home.

Hearing the name "Massa God" got me thinking: *Who was this Massa God, and why was he not sleeping? Did Massa God never sleep because he was watching out for Dake and everyone else to make sure things went right? Did that mean he wouldn't sleep until Dake got his money in full? Surely he couldn't stay awake night and day. He had to sleep at some point.*

This Massa God sounded like a very good man. I wanted to meet him. I wanted to know him.

I continued to think about Massa God long after Dake left, and somehow I concluded that he was my mother's boss, who owned the tobacco plantation across the river. My mother's boss was Mass Bob, and I thought he was really important because he had a Jeep and employed a lot of people. Other than that, I didn't know why I thought Mass Bob could be Massa God.

My father drove a tractor for his boss, Mr. Terrier, who also had a number of people working for him, but I had never thought of him as being Massa God, even though he and Mass Bob were both rich and White, or at least could pass for White. They were considered very important men. Maybe it was the similarity between the names Mass Bob and Massa God. I'm not sure I'd ever seen either Mass Bob or Mr. Terrier; I just knew they were rich and, therefore very important from the way people talked about them.

I made up my mind to find Massa God to see if he was all that Dake had said he was. I wanted to go to the tobacco plantation to spy on Massa God, to watch how he treated his employees. If he treated them nicely, I was going to be his friend. But if he yelled and screamed and ordered them about, I wouldn't have anything to do with him. If Massa God passed my test, I was going to help him do his work. I was going to ride around with him in his Jeep and help him pass out pay envelopes to his workers.

I begged my mother to take me to work with her, but she refused to take me, no matter how much I begged and pleaded. She couldn't understand my request, and I of course couldn't explain the real reason. The plantation was about a mile or two away, across the main road, down a long hill, and across the Rio Minho River. It was no easy journey for a child, and certainly no place for a child either. I eventually gave up on the idea of finding Massa God on the tobacco plantation.

Shortly after I heard about Massa God from Dake, Yvonne and I started kindergarten at the Content Basic School, which was run by the United Brethren Church. There I learned more about Massa God. Our young teacher, Sister Betty, taught us the basics of reading, writing, and math. My favourite part of the day was when she read to us. She read us fairy tales and children's stories from around the world.

And she read us Bible stories too. The first story she read to us was about Adam and Eve. While telling us the story, she mentioned the name God. I was shocked to discover that she knew about him.

I blinked in surprise. *You know God too?*

But as the Bible stories continued, I gathered that his name was not really Massa God.

He's not no Massa God, I thought quietly but confidently. *His name is God, Lord God, Lord God Almighty. Lord is a higher form of mister. God is his first name, and Almighty his surname.* I had a first and last name, so God had one too.

In time, I learned from the Bible stories that God lives in heaven, created the world and everything in it, made the first man and woman—Adam and Eve—in his own image, and that every human being, including me, came from Adam and Eve.

Sister Betty didn't just read the Bible stories. As she told us the stories, she also used an easel board on which she placed pictures of the sun, moon, stars, animals, and the various characters as aids. Each story came in its own little box with its respective characters and other visual aids to help us understand the stories better.

As she told us the stories, she explained the nature of God: "God is good, and he doesn't like evil."

I said, "So am I. So do I. You're doing good, God." I gave God a big checkmark, just like Sister Betty gave us whenever we got our letters and math right.

"God is love," she said, "and he wants us to love everyone."

"I'm love too. You're doing great, God," I said, and I gave him another big checkmark.

Sister Betty said that God told Adam and Eve not to eat the fruit from the tree of the knowledge of good and evil or they would surely die. When they did anyway, I expected them to drop dead right there and then, so I waited with eyes and mouth open wide. When they didn't die, I asked myself, *Bev, did your friend lie when he told Adam and Eve they would surely die if they ate that fruit?* This bothered me a lot. I didn't want to say he'd lied, but I couldn't give God a checkmark for telling the truth. Adam and Eve did not surely die.

I later learned that Adam and Eve didn't die there and then because God hadn't meant that they would die right away but that they would eventually die rather than live forever in the Garden of Eden. But that answer didn't satisfy me.

Sister Betty told us Bible stories about Abraham, Isaac, Jacob, and Jesus. I remember reasoning that God chose Abraham because he was searching for a higher God. According to my interpretation, Abraham looked around and saw people doing wicked things, such as sacrificing their children to their gods, and he said to himself, "This can't be right. This is so gross." Abraham gagged at the sight and smell of a human being burning on an altar and said, "This is wickedness. This is murder. What kind of a god would demand human sacrifice? What kind of god would be happy with the slaughtering of humans? There must be a higher God, one who doesn't require such a terrible sacrifice and is repulsed by the idea of murdering innocent children."

I imagined Abraham looking up to the sky, asking, "Is there a higher God up there, one who really cares about people and what's going on here on Earth?" As a result, God spotted Abraham in the crowd of people on Earth and called him out of Mesopotamia to start a new nation.

When Sister Betty told us another Bible story about God asking Abraham to sacrifice his son Isaac to him, my line of reasoning was thrown into a tailspin. In shame, sorrow, shock, and disbelief, I followed Abraham and Isaac up Mount Moriah. My friend wasn't perfect after all. I had learned that one of the things that set God apart from the other gods in the Old Testament was that he didn't demand human sacrifice.. Now it seemed he was just like the other gods. But God redeemed his reputation when he sent an angel to stay Abraham's hand at the last minute and instead provided a lamb in the thicket. *Whew!* I thought. *That was close, but what a relief!*

I then found the story of Jacob cheating his brother out of his birthright unjust.I expected God to step in and make things right, but he didn't. Things continued like this for weeks, with me evaluating God and giving him checkmarks, until Sister Betty got to a story in Exodus. Imitating the voice of a character in the story, she read aloud, "Who is on the Lord's side?"

I must have been off searching the skies for signs of God as I normally did when she was telling Bible stories. The question jolted me back, and I felt an overwhelming desire right there and then to jump across an imaginary line to be on the Lord's side. Sometime earlier, I had discovered that the words "good" and "evil" were close to the words "God" and "devil," so I'd made a list of all the things that were good, such as love, truth, peace, and justice, and put them under God, and I wrote the opposite of these qualities under the devil. My imaginary line was drawn between the two lists. I never thought I was on the evil side, but I wanted to make it clear once and for all where I stood. I had checked God out and was now ready to be his friend.

In response to the question, I drew that line on the ground and was about to jump across it to be on the Lord's side when a voice called out from above, "Are you sure? Are you sure you've learned everything there is to know about God? You know what they say, 'Look before you leap.'"

"I know I don't know everything about God," I replied to the voice, "but whatever information is coming later will have to align with what I heard before. God can't be love, truth, et cetera, and be the opposite things at the same time. Besides," I added, "even if he's not 100 percent perfect, someone so good can't be all that bad. I want to jump now."

The voice persisted. "What if God says you don't belong?"

"Then I'll undo the buttons on my uniform and ask God to look inside my heart. I'll just ask God to look inside my heart and tell me what disqualifies me. He wants a clean heart, and I know my heart is clean. He'll jeopardize his whole policy of truth and justice if he says I don't belong."

"What if he still says you don't belong?"

"That wouldn't be fair." I thought it through some more and then continued with my response. "That would mean there's a higher God above him who is fair. You're holding me up. I want to jump now."

I jumped on the Lord's side, looked up to heaven, and said, "Look, God, look at me. I'm over here. I'm on your side. I'm on your side, God. I'm on your side. I want to be a Bible person too. And I want my *own* Bible story!"

"What *is* a Bible person?" the voice asked.

"When God speaks to you or angels visit you, or a prophet says to you, 'Thus saith the Lord,' then you can smile because you're a Bible person. You're on Bible camera."

Even though Sister Betty displayed the Bible characters on the easel board, I took no notice of the fact that they weren't of my race or gender. "Bible people are *my* people. Sister Betty says, 'Birds of a feather flock together.' So I flock."

Not long after that, while Sister Betty was reading us another Bible story, I looked up to see a ladder going up to heaven. The ladder stood near the acacia tree by the church, close to the school. On the ladder was a host of Bible people clad in rustic clothes that looked as though they'd been buried under the earth for a long time and were just dug up. They seemed tired and weary.

Once again, the voice asked, "What is the meaning of this?"

"They're wrapping up the Bible. They're wrapping up the Bible. The Bible people are going home," I said.

Abraham was set to cross over the threshold of some invisible door in the sky, as if stepping on an airplane. As I watched them, Bev jumped out of my body and ran up to the ladder, shouting, "Abraham! Abraham! Wait for me!" He turned and looked down at her. Suddenly, Bev felt empty and naked because she didn't have a Bible story. She hadn't done anything with God to qualify her to stand on the ladder.

"Abraham, wait for me!" she said. "I have to find God and get my Bible story, and then I'll come back!"

Then I saw Bev run away from the ladder—which vanished—and come back to class.

After seeing Abraham and the host of Bible people on the ladder, I became more determined to find God and get my own Bible story. I invited him to come to Jamaica and give me a Bible story, and I waited.

In the meantime, I occupied my mind by thinking about what my story would be. I asked myself what I hated the most. After careful contemplation, I decided that what I hated most were spirits. I believed spirits were dead people buried in the ground. They were *duppies* (Jamaican for ghosts). Their flesh had rotted, and only their skeleton was left. They climbed out of their graves wearing long, black, and sometimes white gowns. They could appear and disappear at will. The devil was their leader, and they were evil. They whispered bad things in people's ears and made sport of us because we couldn't see them. They'd tell Tom to hit Dick, then ask Dick if he was going to take that from Tom. In this way, they got them to fight each other. Then they'd laugh their bones off because Tom and Dick had no idea what was really going on.

On the other hand, God made flesh people—human beings and angels—in his own image. Therefore, God was of flesh and the leader of people with flesh. I didn't like spirits because they were evil, and I was sure God didn't like them either. Jesus drove unclean spirits out of people in the Bible, and God said flesh people should separate themselves and not touch the unclean thing. I made up my mind that for my story, I was going to fight spirits, not people.

On one occasion when my mother was combing my hair outside, she left to get a brush or something from inside the house. When she returned, she heard me telling off a lady, saying, "You're mean. You're mean. You're not nice." She asked me who I was cussing. I replied that I'd been cussing the lady going across the field with a little girl.

"What lady? What little girl?" she asked, looking where I was pointing. "There's no one there!" My mother saw neither the lady nor the little girl.

As they'd passed by, the girl had looked at me sadly, as if she wanted to come and play with me, but the lady was being mean to her. I called out and asked her if she wanted to come and play, but the lady grabbed the girl's hand and quickly pulled her away. She was a mean lady. My mother told me to stop making up stories, because no one was there. "They just went by me and didn't stop to crawl under the fence," I insisted. "They walked right through it. They walked through the fence! They didn't bend down or climb over it."

A look of fear had crossed my mother's face. "Bev, what you're seeing are not human beings. They are spirits, and they can harm you."

I guess that was when my first opinion of spirits was born.

But that wasn't the only incident. The lady and the little girl might have been a vision, because I can now interpret it in light of things that happened to me later in life. But at the time I had no way of knowing this. Still, I was puzzled about how or why they went through the fence.

I also recall seeing my mother giving birth to three hearts—what I now know was a vision. She was assisted by a short, old lady with long, grey hair flowing down her back. My mother was in much pain as one by one she delivered each heart, which the lady cleaned with a cloth and stacked one on top of the other. The hearts were spongy and looked like the size and texture of soft *bammy*, a local round flatbread made from cassava, only they were made from flesh.

More of my mother was exposed to me than I wanted to see, so I ran away, covering my eyes and saying, "This is out-of-order-ness! This is out-of-order-ness! (inappropriate). I don't want to see it. I don't want to see it." I was convinced for a long time that I had to keep this a secret because I would have gotten into trouble for seeing something I wasn't supposed to. Only when I got older did I realize that this couldn't have really happened.

Once when I was sick in bed, I woke up to see my mother sitting in the doorway, keeping guard. I called out to her to let her know that I was awake, but she didn't respond. Out of the corner of my eye, I glimpsed the misty form of something in the shape of a human standing under some pictures of Jesus and Mary. I rubbed my eyes to clear them and tried calling my mother again, and before I could do anything else, the misty form was over me. I fought until I found myself slipping into unconsciousness, or sinking inside the mattress—that's how I understood that experience then. When I regained my strength, I jumped off the bed in anger and shouted at my mother, telling her that she had let the man get away.

"What man are you talking about?" she asked with great concern.

"The man I was fighting," I replied angrily. "I was screaming for you to come and hold him so I could beat him up, but you didn't come."

"You were dreaming. I was sitting here the whole time. There's no one here but you and me, and I didn't hear you calling me."

"I wasn't dreaming. I could you see you sitting in the doorway, and he was standing beside you, right under those pictures." The pictures were of the sacred heart of Jesus and Mary holding the baby Jesus.

"If you weren't dreaming, then where is the man now?"

"He went through the back door."

My mother looked at the back door. We both knew it was always locked, but I kept staring at it, because I still had the feeling that the man had gone through the locked back door.

These experiences might have had an impact on my title for a Bible story, but I can't say for sure, because I don't remember if they happened before or after I chose my name and the title of my story. But I remember saying, "I know I'll be bumping into a spirit sooner or later. My name is the Spirit Fighter, and that's what my Bible story will be called: *Bev, the Spirit Fighter*." I knew I couldn't kill spirits by myself, because they could vanish. I didn't know where they were when they did that, but God could see them. He knew how to get them out of "vanishment," and together we would eradicate them.

I wondered why David and the other Bible people never thought about killing spirits, since spirits are the root of all evil. If they had killed spirits, or if spirits were dead, it would be much easier for humans to be good. We wouldn't have them around whispering hateful things to us and causing us to do bad things, not realizing the spirits are messing with our minds.

I went around telling kids at home and play how I was going to kill spirits. "You can't kill spirits," they said, laughing. "They're already dead."

"Then I'll dead them again, and this time it will be for good," I'd say.

Still, they laughed at me. I couldn't let them know that God was my secret weapon against spirits. I couldn't tell them God was coming to Jamaica to help me kill spirits. In the Bible stories, Jesus cast out evil and unclean spirits, so it seemed to me that God, Jesus, and everyone around me didn't like them. God said to come out from among them and not touch the unclean thing (2 Corinthians 6:17). What was the unclean thing? The spirit was the unclean thing.

Sister Betty said God sees and knows where we are and what we do at all times. She taught us Psalm 121:4, which says, "*Behold, he that keepeth Israel shall neither slumber nor sleep.*" I thought that was impossible. God needed to sleep. He'd ruin his health if he kept this up. Nobody could stay awake all day and all night. He'd get tired. I wasn't sure God could see and know what I was doing all the time, because no one had eyes powerful enough to see into every nook and cranny of the world.

The idea of God being aware of what everyone was doing, no matter where they were, didn't leave me. I noticed how the sun crept into every nook and cranny in my house, even when the doors and windows were closed during the day. That got me thinking that the sun must be God's right eye—his daytime eye—that's how he could see and know everything. Then I thought that the sun couldn't really be his eye but was more like his camera eye. I didn't think of the telescope, because the camera was the device I was most familiar with. God sat behind his sun camera on top of Mount Sinai, above Israel, just below heaven, and looked at the world.

And the moon was his left eye, the eye he used at night. He put his left eye and the left side of his body to sleep during the day, and his right eye and the right side of his body to sleep during the night, and that's how he got some sleep and watched the world at the same time.

That solution put my mind to rest about God's health—at least until one day when my cousin Errol, who was about to join his parents in England, said to me, "Bev, do you know that when the sun goes down in Jamaica, it rises in England? It rises in different countries at different times."

"What?" I sighed heavily as I heard this. Just when I thought I had God's sleeping pattern solved, I had to start worrying about the condition of God's health all over again. "God isn't getting any rest at all. As soon as I have God figured out, he moves to another level and I have to start figuring him out all over again."

Sister Betty continued her daily Bible stories, along with fairy tales and other stories. I knew the fairy tales weren't real. Errol told me so when I started school. That's why when Hansel and Gretel got lost in the forest, I felt sorry for them, but I knew they weren't real people. Errol said they were characters in a story made up from someone's imagination to entertain. Errol and my older cousins told me this because they had gone through basic school and were now in big school at Four Paths Primary, a mile or two away. They said the Bible stories were real.

When Sister Betty told the story of Joseph and his coat of many colours, it was so long that she left off where Joseph was taken out of the pit and sold to the Ishmaelite caravan, with the intention of continuing the story the next day. I went home and told my maternal grandma, Ya Ya, that something really bad had happened to Joseph. This startled her.

"D'you mean something bad has happened to Miss Dinah's Joseph?"

"No, no, no!" I stomped my feet.

"Miss Agnes's Joseph?"

"No, no, no! The *Bible* Joseph. His brothers threw him in a hole. Then they took him out and sold him to strangers. Now they're going home to tell their father that a wild animal killed him and ate him up."

"Bev, that story happened a long time ago. You nearly let me fall off my chair thinking that this was news."

"Well, I just heard about it today, so it's news to me."

Thereafter, to avoid confusion, I said Bible Joseph, Bible Abraham, or just Bible people, to avoid getting them mixed up with the people in my community who had similar names.

As I continued to listen to Sister Betty's daily dose of Bible stories, I became more and more frustrated. Almost all the stories seemed to occur in Israel. Sister Betty said God created the heavens and the Earth. If he created the world and everything and everyone in it, why did he focus only on Israel? The older people in my community said, "Don't question God," but the more I learned about him, the more questions I had about and for him. It was as if question marks kept popping up out of my head—*boing, boing, boing*—as if the hairs on my head were sprouting or curling into that very shape.

If God created heaven and the whole Earth, why wasn't Jamaica in the Bible stories? Wasn't Jamaica part of the Earth? If God knew everything, didn't he know Jamaica? Why didn't God say anything about Jamaica in the Bible stories? And if he didn't know Jamaica, how was he going to know *me*?

I couldn't stand it anymore. I looked up to the sky, raised one eyebrow, and asked, "You don't know Jamaica, God?"

I asked the people around me if they thought God knew Jamaica. "Sure," they said. "He knows everywhere in the world."

"Do you think he knows me personally?"

"Yes," they replied. "He knows everyone."

These responses did nothing for me. If God knew Jamaica, then he saw it only out of the corner of his eye, his peripheral vision, because he was just too focused on Israel. And as for God knowing everyone in the world—I knew there were lots of ants living in my yard, but that didn't mean I knew each of them personally or could tell them apart. When God looked down on us from Mount Sinai, we must have looked like a bunch of ants scurrying around. Even if I was an agitated ant, running all over the place, waving my hands frantically at God. Did he know my name? Did he know that I existed? Did he know me the way he knew Moses, David, and all the other Bible people?

As if the distance between Jamaica and Israel wasn't far enough, Sister Betty said God was invisible. We couldn't see him, but he could see us from heaven, way up in the sky. I looked up, and the word "invisible" sounded so big and long that it filled up all the space between me and the sky. It just kept on going—*invisible*—up, up, up, standing between me and God. This big word threatened to keep me from ever seeing and hearing God up close and personal like Adam, Noah, Abraham, Moses, and the others did.

Invisibility threatened to keep me from ever seeing my friend. I wanted a relationship with God like Abraham and Moses and the others to whom God spoke directly had. The idea of a long-distance relationship with an invisible God didn't sit well with me. I began to mumble and grumble.

"Sister Betty, she come tell me God is invisible and that we can't see him with the naked eye. God isn't invisible. My friend is not invisible. He spoke to Adam directly. He spoke to Noah. He spoke to Abraham. If he spoke to them, he can speak directly to me too. He is not no invisible. Come, God. Come to Jamaica and give me my Bible story."

On my way home from Sister Betty's school that day, I stopped in front of the church, where there was a wide-open space. I stared at the sun in order to look God square in his right eye. I reached up into the sky with my right hand, turned, and pulled the sun toward me, forcing God to take his eye off Israel for a while and look at me. I called out quietly, "Over here, God; look over here."

When I felt I had his full attention, I said, "I'm right here, God. Look at me and see where I live in Jamaica. Now climb down Mount Sinai and come to Jamaica and give me my Bible story." I pictured God climbing backward down Mount Sinai. In my mind, a mountain is a huge triangular hill. I lived on the Vere Plains in Jamaica. I only saw mountains in the far distance, never up close. "Follow me, God. Follow me with your sun camera and come visit me at my house." Taking no chances before setting off, I said, "God, if you lose sight of me between the trees and sugarcane fields, you can just come to Lane Head where I'm at right now and ask anyone to show you to my house, okay?"

With that, I turned and ran home as fast as I could so God could watch me running all the way to my house and know exactly where I lived, before he turned away to focus on Israel.

The first year in Sister Betty's school, I learned the basics: counting, the alphabet, and so on. I had a really hard time writing the lowercase "a." I could make most letters except that one. Each time I tried, it ended up looking like a sprouting grain of corn, or a tadpole. I sat on the bench and kept trying, but I couldn't seem to get it right. I got down on the floor on all fours and tried to write a bunch of them, but they still wouldn't come out right. Sometimes I got up feeling as if I'd finally succeeded, only to hear someone snickering, "Look at the crab toes. Crab toes, crab toes, crabby, crabby, crab toes running down the gully." I cried, erased everything, and started all over again, only to end up with a similar result—Yvonne or another classmate pointing and laughing, even though their "a" was no better than mine.

Sometimes Sister Betty would hold my hand as I wrote, and the letters would turn out fine, but the moment I started making them on my own, they went upside down, backward, in a long line that began in the top left corner and ended in the bottom right corner, looking like a bunch of one-legged crabs running downhill on a slant.

One day I became so frustrated with writing the lowercase "a" that I went outside to cool off. I don't remember if I was talking to God or simply wondering why I couldn't make the letter "a" correctly, but I vividly remember a voice saying, "You're trying too hard. Relax when you write." I thought "trying too hard" meant I was pressing too hard on my pencil and "relax" meant I should press gently. I obeyed the voice, and my next attempts were successful. The letter "a" improved thereafter. That was probably the first time I heard Sweet Breeze.

The second time I heard the voice was the day I had a very itchy nose and a cough. The voice said, "You're going to have respiratory problems when you grow up."

I'd never even heard the word "respiratory" before, let alone known its meaning. I was quizzically repeating the word in my mind when I saw a picture, or rather a vision, of my respiratory system. I responded with an understanding "Oh." Later, as an adult, when my doctors told me I had upper respiratory problems—allergies and the like—my mind went back to the time I first heard the word from Sweet Breeze.

The voice spoke to me so often that he seemed a natural part of my life. I assumed everyone had their own Sweet Breeze talking to them. I never questioned who he was. I just named him Sweet Breeze because he always arrived with a sweet breeze, stirring the air above and around me. He seemed to know everything about me and where I was and even where I would be, so I assumed he was a part of me. Sometimes when I played marbles with my relatives and friends, we'd end up arguing and fighting. I'd march off angrily and sit on the tree swing in Dake's yard and I would feel Sweet Breeze coming down like a feather, cool as usual. I would laugh and say, "How did you know I'd be here? I didn't even know I'd be here."

By the second year in Sister Betty's school, we were reading and writing. One of our writing tasks was to practise writing letters to someone. Yvonne and I liked to write letters to her mother, Auntie Bea, in England, asking her for a doll for each of us. There was excited talk among the girls at the school about a doll in England that could walk and say "Mama." The doll's name was Holly Gloucester. Our letters to Auntie Bea were pretend, but the thought of owning such a doll had Yvonne and I walking on cloud nine, dreaming. We fell over each other laughing as we imagined ourselves holding the doll's hand and walking around with it, hearing it call us "Mama." "Mama," we said to each other over and over, mimicking the doll as we rolled on the ground, laughing. We found it funny that someone, or something, could call us Mama.

We took one of our letters home and begged Ya Ya to put stamps and the proper address on it and mail it for us. Ya Ya threw them out and said, "Bea is busy working hard. She has no time or money to waste on foolish things like dolls."

I asked Sister Betty if I could mail a letter to God. She said, "No, but you can pray, and he will hear you." So I started praying to God, asking him for the doll and asking him to drop it off somewhere in the grass up at Top Yard, where I played every day. I didn't have enough faith to ask for the doll I really wanted. I told God he didn't have to send the expensive Holly Gloucester doll—I'd be satisfied with any doll, just as long as it had hair that I could comb and style.

Every day, after my prayer, I went parting the bushes at Top Yard, looking for the doll I believed my friend God was going to throw down from heaven for me. I waited expectantly on God for my big orders: one Bible story and one doll. The doll he could throw down from heaven or give to Gabriel to place in the bushes for me, but God would have to come in person to give me my Bible story.

My paternal grandmother bought me a doll, and that sort of took care of my request. I say "sort of" because I was glad I'd finally gotten a doll, but it had no hair, and I wanted one with hair that I could comb and style. I now directed all my efforts into waiting on God to bring me my Bible story.

As I learned more about God through Sister Betty's Bible stories, I imagined him moving down the timeline, giving out Bible stories, and when he got to my time, it would be my turn. I desired to be a Bible person, but I wasn't fond of the clothes Bible people wore. Their clothes looked as if they'd been made from coarse, striped canvas. I loved their sandals, though, and even pictured myself wearing them.

What fascinated me most about the Bible people, despite their attire, was the light I saw in my mind surrounding them. This light wasn't so much a halo but an inner glow that radiated outward and was reflected on their faces. I envied them this light. I called it "Sabbath in Jerusalem." When I found God and received my Bible story, I too would have my Sabbath in Jerusalem light.

I had a feeling God was going to show up at my house in the evening, in the cool of the day, because that was when he showed up looking for Adam. In the evenings I would run out the gate and stand in the middle of the road to check if God had made it to Lane Head, the intersection where my street, Content, met the York Town main road. I feared the kids who lived up the lane would get to see God before I did when he asked for directions to my house. I was the one who'd invited him to Jamaica, not them. I should see him first.

I imagined Sharon Tyndale or Junie Bobbington coming down the lane, holding God's hand, skipping, smiling, and talking with him. They'd get to my house and say, "Be-ev, guess who's he-eere? God is here to see you. God asked me for directions to your house, so I accompanied him here." The next day they would brag at school. "Bev, you may have called God, but I saw him first." I wanted to have the pleasure of seeing God first, so every now and then I'd leave whatever game I was playing to run out the gate and check on God's progress.

I wanted to see God as soon as he turned the corner at Lane Head. I was going to run up the lane to meet him, take hold of his hand, and say happily, "I knew you'd come. I knew you'd come. They said you wouldn't, but I knew you would." No one actually told me that he wouldn't come, as I never mentioned a word about inviting God to my house to anyone. I was afraid they'd try to talk me out of it with discouraging remarks, jeers, and laughter, saying things like, "God is busy taking care of the universe. Who do you think you are that God should put his important work on hold just to come see you?"

I was not old enough to go to Israel to visit *him*, so he would come to Jamaica to visit *me*. From what I'd learned about him, I believed he would come, and when he did, I planned to do a joyful dance I called the God-knows-me dance in celebration of his arrival. If I were living in Israel, I'd go to Mount Sinai every day after school and walk back and forth, back and forth at the base of the mountain, saying, "Know me, God. Know me. Know me, God. Know me," until God looked down and saw me and knew me. If after doing this repeatedly for a long time God still refused to come down to talk to me, I'd stop going there. Then God would miss me without even knowing why. One day he would say to Gabriel, "Gabriel, something is missing from my day, but I can't place my finger on it. Something used to happen around this time of the day, but I can't figure out what it was."

After giving it some thought, Gabriel would say, "Oh, I know what's missing. It's three-o-clock Bev. In the afternoons, Bev used to come by this time every day looking for you, hoping you'd know her, but I guess she's given up on you because you didn't go down and talk to her." Then God would be curious to know more about me. He would ask Gabriel to go and find me so he could know who I am.

The buses went by Lane Head every day at a fixed time, blowing their distinctive horns from afar, alerting people to their arrival so that their prospective passengers could catch them in time to travel to May Pen or Spanish Town or Kingston. Sometimes a bus would break down or just be running late, and you'd hear one adult say to another, "Hey, wait a minute, how come I didn't hear the three o'clock Vere Liner, or the one o'clock Clarendon Comet bus go by today? Did you hear it? I wonder what's wrong. I hope it didn't break down again or, worse, get into an accident."

People missed hearing the bus horns whenever they didn't show up on time. That's how God was going to miss me going back and forth at the foot of Mount Sinai, shouting in the air, "Know me, God. Know me." Curiosity would get the better of him, and he'd try to find out who I was and why I'd stopped visiting his mountain. But I didn't live in Israel. I lived in Jamaica. And there I waited and waited and waited some more. I looked up to the sky umpteen times a day, saying, "God, it's me again. It's me, Bev, Bev from Content. You don't know me yet? When are you going to come and give me my Bible story?"

Although each day went by without God showing up, I wasn't disappointed. Frustrated, maybe, but not disappointed. I clung to the belief that he was coming the next day. Some evenings I sat at the gate waiting and singing. Then one day as I waited, I was tapping my feet, clapping, and singing a song called "Satisfied," which speaks of having new hands and feet.

> *I looked at my hands,*
> *My hands looked new*
> *I looked at me feet and they did too.*[1]

In the middle of my song, a voice burst in, "Are your hands really new? Are your feet new?"

I looked at my hands and feet, and they were the same old hands and feet, full of scars and bruises. "No, but God is going to send Gabriel to make them new before he comes, because God doesn't like spots or blemishes. He likes perfect skin, and so do I, but there's nothing I can do to make it new."

Between the ages of five and seven, on Saturday evenings I'd go down the road to Mr. Brown's Sabbath School to learn more about God and sing songs to him. When I'd return home, my mother would often say, "Bev, you must be very hungry and thirsty now."

"Yes," I'd reply, "I'm hungry and thirsty, but my belly is full."

"What kind of nonsense is that? You're hungry and thirsty but your belly is full?"

"It's a strange feeling. Although I'm hungry and thirsty, I'm also full. I sing and clap and dance, doing the actions to the songs. All that exercise made me thirsty and hungry, yet somehow I'm strangely full. My praises to God made my belly full."

Then the next day I'd go to my church and praise God in the morning in Sunday school and church service and then in the evening service, learning about God and singing his praises while I waited on him.

I was still in the process of waiting on God when Pastor Eddie announced in church one Sunday, "God is sitting on his throne up in heaven, writing down everyone's name and their sins in his big book."

God must be writing with a pencil that has a big eraser to erase sins when we ask for forgiveness, I thought. I pictured God dressed in his pearly white robe, sitting on his throne behind the sun—his right camera eye. There was a huge desk in front of him on which he wrote and erased sins in his very big book. He heard and saw me telling a little white lie, looked at his watch, wrote my name: Bev, Howells Content, York Town, Clarendon, Jamaica, and the date followed by the sin: *told a lie at 4:00 p.m.* Later, when I asked for forgiveness during my bedtime prayers, He said, "Drat! I wasted my time writing that down." And out came his big eraser.

I wasn't much of a liar. I was just very creative when it came to wriggling my way out of a spanking. I had a sweet tooth and would often steal a penny or two from my parents, hiding it under a cup or a saucer in the cabinet for a few days. If they didn't miss it, I'd run off to the shop and buy sweets. I reasoned that it wasn't really stealing if it wasn't missed, but my conscience said otherwise. That was part of why I worried about God being able to see everything.

Later, when the deed was long in the past and I didn't have to worry about being punished, I'd walk up to my mother, smiling. When she'd ask, "What are you smiling about?" I'd say, "Remember when I said so and so? Well, it wasn't quite so and so." She too would laugh and simply say, "Confession is good for the soul."

Thinking about my pastor's words, I said, "God, you're not in the Bible story business anymore? Pastor says you have a new job writing sins down in a big book. What kind of a job is that? What's happened to you? You used to be a God of action. You used to move about with Adam, Abraham, and Moses. How can you be content sitting there all day and night, writing and erasing sins? It's a boring job, just writing and erasing sins. One of these days, you're going to get so bored that you'll lean back on your throne, put your pencil in your mouth, your hands behind your head, and absentmindedly dangle your foot below the sun. I'll see your foot in your sandal and shout, 'I see you, God! I see you. You're trying to hide from me in invisibleness, but I see you.'"

I smiled to myself when I envisioned God quickly pulling his foot up as I shouted, "It's too late. I see your foot, and it proves you're not invisible. You're real. Why don't you come to Jamaica and give me my Bible story?" But God never slipped up on his new job or his invisibleness.

I wondered if God had gotten older and couldn't move around as much as before. "God, even if you're no longer in the Bible story business, still come to Jamaica to see me. Come call my name and make me laugh."

I was standing at the gate one afternoon, craning my neck to see if God was coming down the lane, when Sweet Breeze said to me, "Surely you must know by now that your friend is never going to come down the lane." That didn't deter me one bit.

"He's going to come. He's going to come. He's going to come, 'cause he's my friend. It's just taking him a long time to get to my house because Bible people don't seem to like travelling by train or plane or bus or car. I don't know why, but they don't seem to go for things like that. They only like to travel by camels, chariots, or horses. Those things don't go too fast."

I tried to picture by what means of travel God would arrive at my house. I didn't imagine him riding a chariot or a horse or a camel, because it would cause quite a stir in Jamaica and on my street to see someone riding a camel or a chariot. No chariot. No horse. And certainly no camel. God didn't want that kind of attention. He'd travel incognito to Lane Head. He was very independent; he would walk all the way.

"He's walking all the way from Israel to Jamaica. That's why it's taking him so long," I said to Sweet Breeze. "I see God stopping under a tree somewhere between Israel and Jamaica, but closer to Jamaica. He says, 'Bev, hold on. I'm coming. I'm tired from all this walking. I didn't realize Jamaica was so far away from Israel.' God says he's going to cook his supper under the tree and rest there for the night. Then he's going to set out for my house first thing in the morning, after breakfast."

I managed to continue waiting for God by telling myself there were a lot of people waiting also, with different prayer requests. Maybe God was simply going down the line, answering each one, and he would get to me when my time came. I would wait my turn.

I waited and waited, then waited some more. It seemed my time would never come. "God," I said over and over, "don't you know me yet? It's me, Bev. Bev from Content. It's full time you know me."

One day after much patient waiting, I ran onto the street and looked up the lane. There was still no sign of God. I turned my eyes toward heaven, and something inside of me exploded. "God! God! You batty naw bun you?" (Translation: "Doesn't your bottom hurt from sitting on your throne day after day?")

I was very mindful of my manners, especially to God, because I feared lightning bolts and thunder would knock me dead. The question popped out without warning, and I couldn't take it back. I walked off in a huff and continued waiting.

"*God is a Spirit: and they that worship him must worship him in spirit and in truth*" (John 4:24). *What? God is a duppy?* The first four words of that sentence from Pastor Eddie's sermon hit me like a bolt of lightning and a jolt of thunder. I was sitting in the front pew, directly in the line of fire, with nothing to shield me from this devastating news for which I was totally unprepared. "God is a … a … spi—? God is a spi—? God is a spi—? God is a …" I choked on the word. I couldn't bring myself to say that word, especially in reference to God. The impact of Pastor Eddie's statement and its meaning to me was so shocking that I could've had a heart attack and collapsed right there and then and no one would've known why.

Sister Betty only said that God was invisible, and that meant we couldn't see him with our eyes. She never said he was a spirit. This was big news. How come I hadn't heard it on the BBC World News from London? I felt like a mother hen, comfortably perched on a tree limb, suddenly being knocked featherless to the ground. Now featherless and wounded, I was trying in vain to find my feathers and stick them back in. I was one angry, naked bird in a terrible state of shock.

Two mourner's benches stood end to end to form the altar of our church, directly in front of the pastor's podium. I had a sudden and overwhelming urge to run up to the benches and bang on one of them with my fist and shout, "Liar! Liar! You're a liar! My friend is not a spirit. That's nastiness. You're nasty. You're unclean." I was way too shy to do any of that. Instead, I just sat there, glaring at Pastor Eddie. *Are you really talking about my friend? My friend is not a spirit.*

I told the children around me that "spirit" was a dirty word, and they shouldn't say it. If they said it, they'd have to get a special soap from God to wash out their mouths to make them clean again. Now pastor was calling my friend God a spirit. Spirits were evil. My friend was not evil. God was no skeleton in a shroud. He had nice, clean skin. He made flesh people in his own likeness and image. That meant he had flesh like we do. What's likeness? What's image? Likeness meant that I had eyes, ears, a nose, and a mouth that made my face look like God's face. Image meant I had a head, hands, and feet that made my body look like God's image.

Why did Pastor have to go and say a thing like that? Why did he have to go and say that God is a spirit? If God is a spirit, and the devil is a spirit, how will I know the difference? When God came to visit me, I could be fighting my very own friend and not even know it. I argued and reasoned silently against the pastor until I was spent. But his words hung in the air like swords stabbing straight through my heart.

I looked around the church for signs of objections from those who had heard Pastor's words, but there were none. I couldn't believe the adults were saying "Amen" in agreement to Pastor calling God a spirit. I simply couldn't believe that not one of them objected or even looked upset. The children seemed even less perturbed. They were making silly faces at each other and happily swinging their legs back and forth while I sat there uneasily, crossing and uncrossing my legs and mumbling and grumbling to myself: *Me not coming back to their church. Me not coming back to their church. Watch and see. Watch and see. Me not coming back to their church. Me quit church. Me done with dem church...* I am done with their church.

I sat there feeling hopeless. Everything was lost—my cause, my friend. Just then, I remembered Sweet Breeze. A surge of hope and joy flooded my being. "I know! I'll ask Sweet Breeze if God is a spirit. Sweet Breeze knows everything. Sweet Breeze," I asked confidently under my breath, "is God a spirit?"

It seemed as if Sweet Breeze's answer was coming from somewhere in the aisle. He paused, as if thinking about the best way to respond, and then said, "Why don't you wait until—"

Assuming he was about to say, "Why don't you wait until you're older, then ask this question again?" I cut him off before he could finish the sentence. I knew that when someone couldn't, or wouldn't, answer a question with a yes or no, it was because the answer was not what the one asking wanted to hear. In desperation, I urged, "Sweet Breeze, is God a spirit, yes or no?"

I waited and waited, but Sweet Breeze didn't respond.

I was expecting an answer, because he had answered the first question, and when he didn't, I realized he didn't want to commit to a yes-or-no answer. Then, seething inward, I got mad—really mad. *So that's why he never showed up!* That's when Bev declared that she wasn't going to wait for God anymore. She was leaving, and she was never coming back to *their* church either, because she was going home. She was going home—not to her mother's house, but to her home behind the sun, where there's a white palace with lots of wide steps leading up to the front door. Bev said she was fed up with this world because nothing was certain. If God was a spirit, then good could be evil and evil could be good, and up could be down and wrong could be right.

That's when Bev popped out of me and stormed out of church. Then, just as suddenly, she turned back. She'd forgotten something. I sat in my seat and watched Bev as she marched angrily up the rostrum. She went behind Pastor's back and yanked the banner she'd made from where it was leaning, folded up in the corner against the wall. She said she didn't want God and his newfound spirit friends to get their hands on her banner of Truth and Justice, so she was taking it to the empty hall in the white palace behind the sun. Furious, she turned again and left the church.

Outside, she unfurled her banner and with determined strides set off for her new home without looking back. She was angry with everybody—angry with Pastor for calling God a spirit, angry with God for letting her down, angry with the congregation for saying amen to Pastor's lie, and angry with spirit for stealing her friend from her and messing up everything.

Bev's intent was to take her banner and put it in the corner of the empty hall in the white palace. After placing it there, she was going to sit outside on the palace steps and ponder why the young man named God had gone to the devil's side when he had so much going for him. As Bev understood the situation on this God-is-a-spirit Sunday morning, God was on his way to her house. He had made it as far as Foga Road, which was less than a mile away from Content, around the corner from Lane Head. He'd met up with spirit and they sold him on the idea of vanishment, as that was all spirits had going for them. And, God went off with them. The palace was empty, but Bev didn't want to say why it was so. She couldn't afford to think of what would happen if the owner decided to come back in his present condition with his new friends. There had to be a safe place somewhere for Truth and Justice.

I don't know how Bev concluded that her banner was completed. From the day I invited God to come to Jamaica and give me my spirit-fighting Bible story, I had started thinking about how best God and I could accomplish my Bible story. I came up with the idea of a banner, perhaps I got the idea from observing the political parties campaigning for votes, or from books or television. I decided that my banner would be made of white satin, emblazoned with the words "Truth and Justice" cut out of gold satin and stitched onto the white background. I probably got this idea from the satin on velvet cloth used to cover the church podium, decorated with a cross and the letters I.H.S. (In His Service).

God and I were going to hold each side of the banner and march around my community. I was going to ask everyone we met, "Are you on the Lord's side or on spirit's side?" If anyone so much as hesitated, even for a moment, it meant they had a trace of spirit in them and were, therefore, unclean. God would snap his fingers and zap that person dead. God had lots of power at his fingertips. I would ask God to perform some miracles to ensure that not a trace of that person, not even his or her bones or ashes, were left to contaminate the Earth. We were going to do this until the environment was rid of spirit and people who talked about spirit.

The main target of our campaign would be the annihilation of spirit. I couldn't see them when they vanished, but God could. He'd get them out of their "vanishment" and burn them to ashes—skeleton, shroud, and all—by snapping his fingers. God would make their very ashes disappear forever so that spirit could never return. When all spirits, and humans with traces of spirit in them, were annihilated, my Bible story would end. God would go back up to Mount Sinai over Israel, and Sister Betty would have my Bible story in a box to read to her students.

But I hadn't made my banner yet. I couldn't ask anyone for the material I needed—they were going say, "We have no money"—let alone tell them why I needed it. I was still in the process of trying to figure out how to procure the material I needed for my banner. I had no clue how Bev got the idea that the banner was completed and leaning against the corner of Pastor's rostrum.

I once told my cousin Errol that sometimes when people bothered me too much, I felt like running away to a safe place behind the sun. He told me the sun was so far away that if I started running at that very moment, I wouldn't get anywhere near it, even when I was old and grey.

Ya Ya was nearby, so I asked Errol, "Old like Ya Ya?"

"Yes, and even older."

"Old like Granny Suzie?"

Errol said, "Yes, even older than Granny Suzie."

Granny Suzie was Dake's mother. She was more than one hundred years old and was probably the oldest member of the community. I thought hard about looking old like Ya Ya and Granny Suzie and decided it wasn't worth the run. The run that would have wasted my entire life and still not gotten me anywhere near the sun.

"Plus," Errol added, "the sun is so hot, you'd get burned up by its heat long before you got anywhere close to it."

But Bev was mad and didn't care to listen to reason. She was on her way to a pure place, where there was no talk of spirit and where Truth and Justice were safe.

Bev got no farther than the pathway between church and "T" Icy's (Aunt Icy's) fence when it started raining and the winds began to blow. Soon there was mud all around Bev. Each time she managed to lift one foot out of the mud to move forward, the other became stuck. Bev was determined, and she was going forward, repeatedly plucking one foot after the other from the mud. But the wind and rain got worse. The mud was getting deeper, and Bev wasn't making much progress.

The wind blew her banner this way and that, because the side that God was supposed to be holding was left unattended, and her arms weren't long enough to hold both sides. The rain was coming down harder and the wind was blowing fiercer. Bev cried and struggled to hold on to her banner and move forward. Her feet continued to sink deeper with each step, and the wind threatened to blow her and her banner away. I felt so sad for Bev but could only watch helplessly as she struggled with her banner.

That was the last time I saw or heard from the Spirit Fighter.

CHAPTER FOUR

Mother Miserable

I dragged myself home from church on what I referred to as Spirit Sunday. That's what I called that dark Sunday when I heard, for the first time, that God was a spirit. I felt lost, rejected, and dejected—but most of all, defeated. God almost made it to my house, but then he went off to join the spirits, leaving his flesh children whom he had created with his own hands, in his own image, and in his own likeness, on their own. What was going to happen to us? Was God going to whisper evil things in our ears too? One thing was certain: I couldn't be friends with a spirit God.

I changed out of my church clothes and into my play clothes, but I didn't feel like playing. I went and sat under the skinny ackee tree that always seemed on the verge of dying but somehow managed to survive. There I pondered, over and over, what could've gotten into God to make him go and do such a thing.

My mother walked by and saw me deep in thought with my hands on my jaw. She came up to me, took one look at my face, and asked, "What's bothering you now?" I didn't answer. I just kept staring ahead. How could I tell her? At my silence, she remarked, "Bev, did your husband die or run off and leave you with ten children to support? My goodness, you can certainly fret and worry yourself. Look at your face! You're old before you're even young!"

I just sat there and let her remarks roll off me. I couldn't tell her what Pastor had said about God; I had a feeling she was going to side with the pastor and say something like, "Bev, Pastor knows what he's talking about." I couldn't stand hearing another adult side with Pastor on the subject of God being a spirit. Sweet Breeze's refusal to commit to a yes-or-no answer on that subject left me feeling so beaten down that I couldn't bear hearing another favourable word about spirit.

As I sat there under the ackee tree, I vowed in secret to never speak with God again or have anything to do with him. I refused to look up to the sky. I couldn't look God in his sun eye. I was so ashamed and embarrassed. "Don't put all your eggs in one basket," I heard the folks around me say all the time. But I was so sure I couldn't lose with God, so I put all in without any reservation whatsoever. And now this!

"How could you do this to me? I'm never going to speak to you again. You told me to come out from among them and to not touch the unclean thing. Now look what you've done. You've gone and joined up with spirit! What is the unclean thing? Spirit is the unclean thing. I'm not speaking to you again, and I'm not going back to your church either." I sat under the tree for a long, long time, rocking back and forth as my thoughts raged on and on.

I became sort of a rebel at church after Spirit Sunday. I avoided Pastor like the plague. Each time I saw him coming my way, I bent down and pretended to tie my shoelace or buckle my shoe. I didn't want him to touch me or speak to me. I wanted to quit church because of Pastor's lie, but I dared not so much as mention a word of that to my parents. I knew that even though neither of them was a churchgoer, they would have none of it. I dared not say out loud, "I'm not going back to church because Pastor is preaching pure lies about God." They would say with shock on their faces, "Say that again. I'm not sure we're hearing right. Say it one more time." Then they would give me something that would send me running off to church faster than my legs could carry me.

So the following Sunday I was off to church—in body, but not in mind or in heart. Pastor led in singing the hymn "We're Marching to Zion." The congregation sang:

Come, we that love the Lord,
and let our joys be known;
join in a song with sweet accord,
and thus surround the throne.

We're marching to Zion,
beautiful, beautiful Zion;
we're marching upward to Zion,
the beautiful city of God.[2]

As their voices reverberated throughout the small church, I sat in my seat and refused to sing along with them, muttering sarcastically, "We're marching upwards to Zion, the beautiful city of God? Just where do they think they're going? I ain't going with them. God is no longer in Zion, his beautiful city. God backslid. God has turned back."

"Backslid" and "turned back" were terms used to describe members who had left the church to go back to their old ways. Those were the only words I knew to describe what I believed God had done to his people and the church, but deserted or defected would have been more apt.

The church was a ship without a captain, and it was floundering. But Pastor and the congregants didn't seem to be aware of this. They continued singing joyfully:

Let those refuse to sing
who never knew our God;
but children of the heavenly King,
may speak their joys abroad.

We're marching to Zion,
beautiful, beautiful Zion;
we're marching upward to Zion,
the beautiful city of God.[3]

You need to stop singing these nice songs about God, I continued arguing. *The church needs to call a meeting. It needs to discuss how to get God to come to His senses and come back to leading His people. But can God still be perfect after running off with spirit? And if and when He does come back, can He be fully trusted again?*

Another Sunday, and the congregation was singing one of those marching hymns. I think it was "Onward, Christian Soldiers." Pastor said, "Let's stand for the singing of the hymn." I flatly refused to stand or sing. Sweet Breeze whispered, "Stand up, soldier!"

I whirled on him. "Me naw stand up! Me naw stand up! And I am not marching either. God has run off with spirit, and the church is carrying on as if nothing has happened. The church doesn't know where God is; therefore, it doesn't know where it's going. I am not following them! I can't wait to get out of here. I can't wait to get out of here. I can't wait to be old enough to quit church for good."

"When will that be?" a voice that seemed to come from inside me asked.

I looked at the floor and noticed that, unlike the younger children such as myself, the feet of the adults and some older children were firmly placed on the floor while they sat in the pew.

"I'm outta here as soon as my feet can touch the floor when I sit on the bench," I answered. From then on, every Sunday I sat on the bench and measured how much I had grown by how close my feet were to the floor, and boy, did I ever grow fast.

Some weeks passed, and just before closing one afternoon, the church was singing another rousing, marching hymn. I think it was "Sound the Battle Cry."

Sound the battle cry! See, the foe is nigh;
Raise the standard high for the Lord;
Gird your armour on, stand firm, every one;
Rest your cause upon His holy Word.

Rouse, then, soldiers, rally round the banner,
Ready, steady, pass the word along;
Onward, forward, shout aloud, Hosanna!
Christ is Captain of the mighty throng.

Strong to meet the foe, marching on we go,
While our cause we know, must prevail;
Shield and banner bright, gleaming in the light;
Battling for the right we ne'er can fail.

O Thou God of all, hear us when we call,
Help us one and all by Thy grace;
When the battle's done, and the vict'ry's won,
May we wear the crown before Thy face.[4]

Before I knew it, I was up, marching and singing right along with Pastor and the adults. Sweet Breeze waited awhile and then asked, "Are you back?"

I responded swiftly, "No, I'm not back. I forgot I was out." I promptly sat back down.

BEHOLD A JAMAICAN INDEED, IN WHOM THERE IS NO SPIRIT

During Sunday night services, just before prayer time, Pastor led the church in prayerful songs with words such as "Spirit of the living God, fall afresh on me" or "Sweep over my Soul." These songs invoked the presence of God, but each time I heard any such songs about to begin, I got out of the church as fast as I could to avoid being contaminated by any drop, or even one iota, of spirit falling on or sweeping over me.

I ran outside and breathed on my hands and used them to "wash" myself from head to toe. That was something children did whenever they accidentally touched or bumped into someone who was supposedly their enemy. Then I lifted my arms, spread them wide like wings, and let the pure breeze from outside rinse me off while I waited for the songs to be finished before returning to my seat.

During the times when I couldn't get outside because of the church "police," who wanted to know how many times I needed to go to the bathroom or get a drink of water, I would duck each time I heard the word "spirit" coming up in a song, so that spirit, and whatever the song was asking spirit to do, would pass over me without touching me.

Pastor said, "God is here. Can you feel him?"

I replied, "Where? Where? Where is he? I don't see him. I don't want to feel him. I want to see him. I want to see him with my two eyes. Where is he? Where is he?" I looked up at the rostrum with crossed eyes, squinty eyes, normal eyes, trying different lenses, all in an effort to pull God out of invisibleness so I could catch a glimpse of him.

I remained in this rebellious mood for some time, but life without God made everything dark and empty. Eventually, I gave up. I needed to speak with God again. I needed to go back to the way things were before Pastor told that dreadful lie on God. I convinced myself that God was not a spirit and started to speak with him again. I told God that Pastor had told a lie on him, saying he was a spirit, and how everyone in the church agreed, but I didn't. I told God that Pastor didn't really mean to lie about him; he just didn't know any better. Spirit, spirit, spirit was all those people seemed to talk about. I explained to God that these Jamaican people talked so much about spirit that they were just having a hard time imagining a world without spirits. Pastor was just confused as a result of all this talk about spirits and their power to vanish into thin air. I took hold of the hands of my friend, Flesh God, resumed talking to him, and my world became bright again.

Pastor said that Moses or Jesus said, "Thou shalt love the Lord thy God with all thy soul, with all thy might, and with all thy strength" (Matthew 22:37).

I said, "I can love the Lord with all my heart, might, and strength, but I want to know if the soul is the same thing as spirit, because if they are one and the same, then I don't have no soul because I most certainly don't have any spirit."

With the return of my relationship with God, I believed God was still on his way to see me. When he came, he'd go to church with me to deliver a sermon that would set the record straight once and for all about this spirit business.

I imagined that I saw God over in the section of the church close to the podium, sitting on one of the pews where Pastor and his family and guest speakers usually sat, and where my primary and junior Sunday school classes were held before the main service on Sunday. There God sat, wearing a dark suit with a white shirt and tie. He wasn't wearing his white robe today, because he didn't want people to recognize him right away. His suit was well ironed with no wrinkles because he was perfect and didn't like spots or wrinkles. The seams on God's pants were razor-sharp. Everyone wore nice, crisp, clean clothes to church on Sundays—their Sunday best. God's clothing was the same or better.

Did God have hairy legs? I wondered. I sure hoped so. I thought it was very funny if men didn't have hairy legs, because I was a girl and I had hairy legs. I peeked at God's legs below the hem of his pants, above his socks, to see if he had hairy legs. And he did.

In all my imaginings of God, I could never quite see God's face clearly, no matter how hard I tried to picture it. And despite our renewed relationship, I still most definitely couldn't picture it. I knew his complexion was a mixture of all the races on Earth, but I couldn't tell the colour of his eyes or hair. I couldn't tell what his nose or mouth looked like either. But I couldn't leave God headless or faceless, so I said he looked like Abraham or Moses and left it at that.

So God came and sat with his legs crossed like the other important men who visited our church. But God wasn't very comfortable, because he was used to wearing white robes instead of pants. And he was *definitely not happy*, because Pastor had called him a spirit. Anyway, God sat there waiting his turn, waiting for the praise and worship and scripture reading to be over so that he could preach. Pastor introduced him.

"Our guest speaker for today is none other than God himself."

That's when God took his sermon papers out of his briefcase and ascended to the rostrum. He stood behind the pulpit, cleared his throat, looked at the audience, and said, "The topic of my message today is, 'I Am Not a Spirit.'"

God began, "Now, there's been a rumour..." He paused for emphasis, looked out at the audience to make sure he had their undivided attention, and continued. "There's been a lot of talk going around here lately that I am a spirit. Well, here I am. See me. Feel me. Touch me. I am not a spirit." He was very nice, of course. He didn't want to say out loud that Pastor was the one who started the rumour. He didn't want to point fingers or cause any embarrassment. He was just there to set the record straight.

I stayed in my seat, trying to be calm and trying my best not to giggle or grin my silly head off when I saw the look on Pastor's face when he heard this from God's own mouth. I knew my friend wouldn't let me down. He wasn't like that.

Up until God-is-a-Spirit Sunday morning, I was a good follower of the Word, learning all I could about God. I followed Pastor's preaching along with what I gleaned from Sister Betty's Bible stories and Sunday school.

Pastor Eddie said, "You cannot serve God and Mammon," and I thought to myself, *Mammon. Mammon. What is Mammon?*

The closest word I could get at to comprehend the meaning of Mammon was mammal. Sister Betty said that the whale was the largest mammal on Earth. I said, "You have nothing to worry about with me on that one, God. I won't serve no whale with you."

Pastor preached that the young women's miniskirts were too short. I turned to look at the teenagers to see if it was true. The teenagers were sitting in their usual place on the back pews behind me; they didn't look pleased with Pastor.

Pastor said, "Fornication is a sin."

I had to think hard about that word too. *Fornication? I don't know what that means. Forn … forn … forn …"* The root word system I used to help me decode big words wasn't working here. The closest word I could come up with was forlorn, from the Christmas carol "Mary's Boy Child": "By and by they found a little nook in a stable all forlorn, and in a manger cold and dark, Mary's little boy child was born."[5] A stable was not a place fit for humans. The word forlorn didn't make any sense in the context of Pastor saying fornication was a sin. A dark, cold manger was not a sin. Only animals lived there, and animals couldn't sin. As much as I hated to abandon my thoughts without coming close to an answer or solution, that one didn't make any sense, so I gave up.

Then Pastor said, "Thou shall not commit adultery."

This was way easier. The root word was adult. I was a child, not an adult, so the word certainly didn't apply to me. I couldn't commit adultery if I was a child. I was about to leave it at that when I heard a voice inside my head imploring me to take a shot at the word. The voice asked, "So what is adultery?" I replied, "It's games adults play on each other, trying to outsmart the other." I turned my attention back to Pastor.

Pastor continued, "the flesh is carnal-minded."

Carnal? He means kernel, I think. He should've said kernel. These Ja-maican people have a way of mispronouncing words. They say carnal when they mean to say kernel. The proper term is kernel-minded. Yvonne was ker-nel-minded; she liked to eat mangoes and guineps all the way down to the seed. She used her teeth to scrape the seeds bald and then chew the guinep seed to a pulp. Then she'd stick her tongue out, covered with the chewed-up pulp, to gross people out. I told her not to do this, because the kernel inside the seed wasn't meant to be eaten. The seeds were meant to be planted, and the juice from the seeds would make her sick. But she didn't listen. She didn't care. She kept on cracking mango and guinep seeds with her teeth and chewing guinep seeds up, because she derived great pleasure from grossing people out. And that made her kernel-minded.

Pastor Eddie said, "The flesh and the spirit are at war with each other."

And I said, "Yes, they sure are."

Pastor went on, "The spirit lusteth after the flesh, and the flesh lusteth after the spirit."

I agreed, because I was flesh and I was definitely at war with spirit. Spirits were at war with humans, whom God created in flesh in His own image and likeness. I could see flesh and spirit on either side of the trench bordering "T" Icy's house and the church property. They were lusting and challenging each other to cross the line and make the first shot. Lusting meant they were taunting and lunging at each other. Flesh was at a dis-advantage, because it couldn't vanish at will and spirit could. Spirit knew that God was on the side of flesh, so they couldn't do to flesh what they would like to do. But they tried anyway, because they had the power to vanish at will. Flesh people needed God to help them fight spirit because they didn't have any magic power.

"Flesh is corruption, and the works of the flesh bring death, but spirit is life." The congregation really warmed up to Pastor's sermon with shouts of "Amen," but I stopped in my tracks. I was with Pastor up to this moment, pretty much agreeing with him, until he said that. He was wrong on that corruption part. I knew that corruption—which the locals called "pus" back then—sometimes oozed out of the cuts and boils on our bodies, but our flesh was certainly not dead, and not all of it was corruption. And spirit was definitely not life. Spirits are devils and the remains of dead people, so spirit is dead. And I hoped God got to my house before I died. I didn't want to be buried in a hole in the ground and become a spirit with a skeleton and a shroud. Then I might end up on the wrong side, because spirits were dead people under black or white shrouds, and the devil was their leader.

Another week and Pastor, his voice growing ever louder, said, "God is coming back for a church without a spot or wrinkle." At first I thought he was talking about clothes, and I wondered how God expected me, or anyone else, to keep our clothes looking freshly washed, starched, and ironed while wearing them. I was in deep trouble with God on this one. Even in my Sunday best dresses, I climbed Mr. Man Man's jimbeline tree to pick the tiny, yellow fruit that children loved because it was sour. And while at church, pretending we were going over to Miss Matty's or Mr. Bogle's water pipe for a drink of water, I would climb or stone their mango trees to obtain the sweet, juicy, fine mangoes. I was so well-known for my climbing that Sa Ma's daughter, Faith, looked at me one Sunday in my crisp, white cotton dress and remarked, "Your mother is really brave to put you in a white dress."

Then I caught on. Pastor was talking about our skin. I looked at everyone's legs and arms, and I seemed to have more spots than anyone around me. I didn't have any wrinkles, but I had many spots in the form of cuts, bruises, blemishes, and scars. Sister Betty's students were always falling down splat on their faces when they ran, bruising their knees and palms—and they ran a lot. I also loved to run, jump, hop, skip, and swim, and my limbs were made for climbing trees, so I was always getting cuts and bruises. I began to worry about my spots and blemishes.

And then it hit me: I didn't have wrinkles, but half the congregation was full of them. I looked at the older members' faces, and I could see that they didn't appear to be the least perturbed by the news that God was coming back for a church without spot, blemish, or wrinkle. On the contrary, they were nodding "Amen" to Pastor, as if they didn't understand the full implications of his message. Didn't they realize Pastor was saying that God was going to leave them behind when He came for His church and found them with wrinkles? Then I thought, *No, no, that can't be right. God can't throw them overboard if they've been serving him faithfully all these years until they've grown old and wrinkly. He can't just walk in and say, "Get out! I don't want you in my church because you have wrinkles." That wouldn't be truth. That wouldn't be justice. Truth is that they've been serving God faithfully all these years until they've grown old and wrinkly. Justice is that they deserved to go to heaven for their faithfulness.* God would have to invent a cream for their wrinkles.

I was certain the older folks didn't like wrinkles either. They simply couldn't do anything about them. So my advice to the older members was, "Stay on board. Stay on board. God can't throw you overboard because you have wrinkles, for then he wouldn't be a God of truth and justice. If he doesn't like spots or wrinkles, he'll just have to invent a cream to make your skin perfect like his."

I told God that since he didn't like spots, he'd have to send Gabriel to touch my scars and spots and make them go away. I didn't know until that day that he didn't like blemishes or spots and wrinkles. I didn't like them either, and I'd love to have perfect skin, but I couldn't make the scars and blemishes vanish. I knew he didn't like animals with blemishes to be offered up as sacrifice to him, but I didn't know that extended to his church.

From then on, I tried my best to avoid getting any more scars or spots on my skin, but the harder I tried, the more they appeared. I got them whenever I played, no matter how hard I tried to avoid it. And I couldn't just sit around and do nothing. I fell off bicycles and bruised my hands, knees, and elbows as I learned how to ride. Yvonne and I were sure we could beat the boys at everything. From bicycle racing to racing them on foot down the road, to swimming and diving, you name it. If it was action, we were into it. And sometimes we ended up with cuts and bruises.

I got a whole bunch of scars and spots. And it didn't help that my skin sometimes broke out for seemingly no reason. Aunt 'Manda said it was because I ate too many sweets. I did eat a lot of sweets, but I couldn't see how that could make my skin break out and leave such ugly spots.

Then Yvonne came up with the idea of each of us taking turns being rolled around the house in an old oil drum we leaned against the wall and sat on. Each one got inside for their turn while the others pushed it all the way around the house. They all seemed to be having fun and squealing with delight, so I could hardly wait for my turn. My turn came, and I got in, expecting a thrilling, fun ride, but to my horror, my stomach and brain started churning, and I began to feel sick. "Let me out! Let me out! My head is spinning and I'm getting sick," I screamed.

"No," Yvonne replied. "Everyone had their turn and completed it. You don't get to get out till you complete your ride around the house." And she continued to roll the drum at full speed. I was nauseated, so I started to climb out of the rolling oil drum, the sharp edges of which were beaten down but raw on the inside. I managed to crawl out, but not before getting sliced on my knee by the edge of the oil drum as I made my not-too-cool exit.

They bulldozed a big tree in my friend Lorna's back yard, across the road from Top Yard and beside Over Yard. We pretended the fallen tree was a horse and rode it like cowboys, whipping it along. The rough bark ripped the skin on my leg. Another scar. It was impossible to have perfect skin.

"God," I said, "I give up trying to have perfect skin. You have to send Gabriel to touch my bruises and scars and make them disappear so that I can have perfect skin like yours. I don't like cuts or scars either, but there isn't much I can do about them."

I imagined Gabriel meeting me on the church lawn. He was barefoot and dressed in white. I ran to meet him, laughing and saying, "I know you'd come. I know you'd come. I know my Bible people would come to see about me."

Gabriel was about to say "Fear not," but I smiled at him and told him, "There's no need to say that. I don't have anything to fear from my people." I took Gabriel's hand as we walked on the grass together. Gabriel smiled at me and touched my scars, spots, and blemishes. They disappeared and I had perfect skin, just like God and Gabriel.

I wished Pastor would stop preaching about spirit and start preaching about God. He preached about the devil and hellfire and worms that didn't die. He preached about Judgement Day and the wrath of God, but none of that bothered me. What bothered me was Pastor preaching about the Holy Spirit or Holy Ghost. He insinuated that God was friends with the Holy Spirit, and that the Holy Spirit resided with God. I didn't care if his first name was Holy. His last name was Ghost or Spirit, so I didn't think the Holy Ghost or Holy Spirit belonged in heaven or with God. I thought he was in the wrong place. I didn't know how the Holy Spirit and I were going to live together in Heaven. We didn't like each other. The Holy Ghost was out to get me. He wore a long, black gown and looked pretty much like the Grim Reaper. He'd stand behind God's throne, constantly on my case, saying, "See, God? Bev told another lie just now. Can I get her now? Can I get her?" God would say, "No, leave her alone. Give her some time. She'll ask for forgiveness soon." The Holy Ghost would stomp his feet and storm off, fuming mad, because God wouldn't let him get me.

I wanted to know more about God, not about the Holy Spirit. Was God married? If God wasn't married, then who washed God's clothes? Who cooked God's food? I could see God's white robes on the clothesline in heaven, blowing in the heavenly breeze and drying in the heavenly sunshine. But I didn't know who washed them. Neither Pastor nor the adults around me ever mentioned if God had a wife, and I didn't think I could dare broach such a touchy subject with any of them. But from what I gathered, it appeared God was single. I put the question to my playmates, most of whom were my relatives. We weighed the evidence, or perhaps the lack thereof. There was no Mrs. God mentioned in the Bible stories, sermons, or conversations. Together, we arrived at the firm conclusion that God wasn't married. So if God wasn't married, how did he do his housework along with his church and universe work? He was very independent and would try to do it all by himself. I didn't think he should have to do his housework too. He should have some time to rest.

Did God go home after church every Sunday to cook rice and peas and chicken or curry goat for his Sunday dinner? Sunday dinner was the most important dinner and the fanciest meal of the week in Jamaica. A lot of hard work went into preparing it. My mother started soaking the peas and seasoning the meat for Sunday dinner on Saturday evenings when she returned from the market. She'd still be cooking dinner when I got home from church. In fact, she didn't finish until around five o'clock in the evening or thereabouts. So, when God got back to heaven all tired and hungry from running to all the churches on Sundays, I wondered if he had to spend all evening cooking his Sunday dinner.

My brother Glen and I were baffled about how God could be present in every church when they all beseeched, requested, begged, pleaded, and invoked his presence at about the same time each Sunday morning and night. We concluded that God took off like a superhero, running to and from one church to another. In order to be present as requested, he just popped in, out of breath from running fast, and said, "Present," and then took off running to the next church. That was tiring work, even for God.

I wondered if Gabriel was the one who washed God's clothes and cooked God's food while God did his important work in the church and the universe. I didn't like doing housework and wondered if Gabriel liked doing God's housework. If Gabriel didn't like doing it, did he have to do it anyway? Could he say no to God? Would God punish him if he refused? Or did Gabriel have the freedom to say yes or no? If God forced Gabriel to do his housework when he didn't want to, wasn't that injustice? If Gabriel was afraid of being punished by God and said yes to housework when he really meant no, was that a sin?

Unlike our parents, God could read minds, so he would know if Gabriel wasn't telling the truth. Apart from the issue of living with the Holy Ghost in heaven, that was the only other drawback of living with God. He would always know what I was thinking, and it made me a bit uncomfortable, because there were times when I wished he *didn't* know.

To help God and Gabriel out with the housework problem, I invented a mother for God; a wife would've been more appropriate, but I thought it safer to give God a mother, because if he wanted a wife, he would have married. Besides, everyone could use a mother. God's mother didn't have a name. She didn't wear high-heeled shoes like the women at church. She wore heavy boots like army boots, because she literally had to put her feet down—stomp them—to get God to listen to her when she told him to take it easy and rest. She wasn't really God's mother, though, because God was older than her. God just let her occupy the role of being his mother, because everyone likes to be pampered once in a while.

God's mother had his dinner ready and waiting when he returned home from church on Sunday afternoons. She said, "God, eat your dinner, then put your pyjamas on and go straight to bed after dinner. You're tired and you need to rest. You spoil those children of yours on Earth too much. Every time they need something, they call on you: 'God, God, please help me, Lord God, have mercy on me.' When they're okay, they forget all about you. Let them learn to stand on their own two feet. Switch them on automatic to make sure no one dies while you're sleeping. Now go straight to bed when you've finished eating your dinner."

God didn't *have* to do what his mother said, but he did it anyway, because he knew she was right. He went to bed and slept for a while, but around seven o'clock at night, the sound of singing from the noisy children and adults of the Content United Brethren Church woke him up. He tossed and turned in bed and finally said, "I can't sleep when those children are singing. If I stay in bed, I won't get any more sleep. Should I stay or go? I won't be sleeping anyway. It's six if I stay and half a dozen if I go. I may as well go down there and enjoy myself with them." So God took off his pajamas, got dressed, snuck out of his bedroom, and came to church. And nobody knew about this except God and me.

After school, my mother yelled, "Bev, come get the water pan and go fetch water and fill the (oil) drum!" We used the drum to store water for household purposes. I was in the middle of playing marbles up at Top Yard, and the game was at its height. I thought I was on a winning streak, but it was probably more of a losing streak, since no one boy, or girl, could beat Yvonne at marbles. We secretly partnered up to try to beat her. I had to win my marbles back before the players called it quits and went home for dinner with my pretty, shiny new marbles.

My mother yelled again. "Bev! Bev! Do you hear me calling you? Don't let me come up there and get you!" At that, I grabbed my marbles and quickly headed for home.

I got the water pan and placed some marbles in one corner of its square bottom. For some strange reason, this pan was known as the kerosene pan. Kerosene is more akin to gas and was used for lighting fires, especially cooking fires, or to power cooking stoves. I didn't really know how the water pan, which once held cooking oil in the shops, came to be known throughout Jamaica as the kerosene pan. Perhaps in times past similar pans held kerosene oil. What I did know was that our parents, like theirs before them, bought those pans from local shopkeepers when they became empty so that we could use them to transport water from the public pipes.

My mother warned, "Bev, I'm sending you to get water, not play marbles. You have to fill the drum before it gets dark. You have to water the flowers too, so don't go to the water pipe and play marbles. Let me see your hands." I put the water pan down and boldly showed her the palms of my hands, hoping she wouldn't ask me to shake the pan or show her the inside.

With a smile for outwitting my mother, I picked up the water pan and continued down the street, grumbling, "God, you're so lucky you didn't have a mother to bother you when you were a little boy playing marbles. You could play marbles all day, and no mother would be yelling out your name, wagging their finger at you, saying 'God! God! Don't let me come up there and get you. God, if I come up there and get you, you won't like it. God, if I have to call your name one more time …' God, you were the luckiest kid in the world." Then I paused. "Wait a minute. God, you didn't have a mother, but you also didn't have any friends to play marbles with."

I pictured God as a little boy in short pants playing marbles every day all by himself until he grew up and started wearing long pants. "Oh my God. God, you were not just an only child, you were *the only* child. There was nobody for you to play with. There were no mothers, so there were no children. You could play marbles for as long as you wished, but you had to play by yourself. That couldn't have been any fun. You had to wait until you grew up and started making angels and people before you had someone to play with. But by then, you were too old for marbles. God, I don't think your childhood was so great after all."

I was getting older, so my share of the housework steadily increased. I traded in the idea of my Bible story and being the mother of an orphanage for the chance to escape to Hollywood, California, to become a cowboy. Cowboys didn't do housework, and they had lots of adventure in the wild, wild west. In the movies, they advised young men to go west. Well, I was a girl, but I was heading out west, whether they liked it or not.

I was growing tired of waiting for a sign that God knew me personally and was keeping his end of the bargain to help me escape to America. While washing the dishes, sometimes I'd snatch up a dish and bang it loudly against the table, a bang for each word, while saying in my mind, *God, this is not Hollywood. This is not California. When are you going to get me out of here?* If my mother happened to be home, she'd yell, "Bev, are you going to break my dishes?" and send a slipper flying in my direction. But I'd duck down like a good cowboy.

Sometimes I thought the roof of the makeshift kitchen separated me from God, so I marched out into the open air and looked up into the sky, moving frustrated lips and gesticulating wildly while reminding God that I was still not in Hollywood, as per our agreement. Sometimes my mother saw me doing this and said, "Look at Alice in Wonderland. Look at her go again. I swear that child is crazy."

I went down to the canal a little distance behind our house to wash the clothes and have some fun in the water. I was there to rinse the clothes, as my mother had taken up having me wash at home under her supervision. This way she could ensure sufficient time was spent on each piece of clothing to guarantee it was clean. She used to let me go washing on Saturdays with Yvonne and the other girls from the community while she went to the market in May Pen. I didn't have much interest in doing the family's weekly laundry by hand. The commercial said, "Dirt can't hide from intensified Tide." So I said, "Tide, do your stuff while I do mine." I put the clothes in the wash pan to soak in New Intensified Tide and ran off to compete in swimming and diving contests or go fishing with the neighbourhood children, including Yvonne.

My mother asked Yvonne to keep an eye on how long I spent washing the clothes. Yvonne promised me she wouldn't squeal on me, but as soon as my mother got home and asked how I did, Yvonne started grinning. "Bev played all day then quickly squeezed the clothes and hung them on the line when she knew it was time for you to come home," she said.

My mother pulled the clothes off the line, and I had to wash them all over again, crying as my tears joined the water in the wash pan. My mother made a career out of cooking, washing, starching, and ironing, and she forced me to follow in her footsteps. I saw only the tears that came rolling down my cheeks each time I heard about or saw housework.

As I stood there on the banks of the canal, looking up to the sky, I said, "God, you're taking so long to know me and get me out of here. How did Abraham manage to get your attention in Ur? Did he find a clearing and dance around in a circle like a wild bird? I'm not above doing that, if that's what it takes."

The sugarcane had just been harvested, and I spotted a recently cleared area in the sugarcane field nearby. In order to get God's attention, I was seriously thinking about imitating the dance of the wild birds I saw on nature shows on television. I pictured God with his sun camera or a telescope looking at Israel, then out of the corner of his eye, he would see me dancing up a storm and zoom in for a closer look at the spectacle. God would laugh and yell, "Gabriel, Gabriel, come quick! Take a look at this!"

Gabriel would go over to God, take one look, and exclaim, "What on Earth is that?" He'd take a closer look and say, "It looks like someone is in distress. She's sending you an SOS. Do you want me to go down to Earth and find out who it is and what her problem is?"

I looked around to see if anyone was in sight. There was no one about, but for fear of being declared insane, I decided against the idea of doing the wild bird dance. So I stood there, gazing up at the sky. Then a voice,

seemingly from inside my head, said, "Bev, the same sun that you're looking at now in Jamaica is the same sun Abraham saw in Ur and throughout
his life." I thought about that for a while. Somehow it gave me hope that
even though I wasn't living in any of the countries mentioned in the Bible, and although Abraham's time was so far removed from my mine, one
thing still connected me to Abraham: the same sun. It gave me faith to
believe there was hope for me yet.

A few years later, my mother got a job in Kingston, and I was forced
to take on 100 percent of the housework. While the other kids played
marbles, I cooked dinner. The food wasn't cooking fast enough for me to
get back to playing marbles with the other children. The fire under the pot
was feeble because of the lack of good firewood, which was getting harder
to find. A marble game was in full swing up at Top Yard, but I couldn't get
back into the game until I'd completed dinner. I had to have dinner ready
before my father got home.

I blew on the firewood to get the fire going so the water in the pot
would begin to boil and I could put the ingredients in. The quality of the
firewood was so inferior—cornstalks, I believe—that they wouldn't burn,
no matter how hard I fanned or blew on them. Overcome with anger and
frustration, I started cursing my fate. *Why me? Why does everyone get to
have fun, while I get stuck with the housework? Why? Why? Why was I born
poor? Why do I have to be cooking dinner when the other children are free to
play marbles?*

At times like that, I cussed and threw things in all directions, then
threw myself on the ground, rolled around in the dirt, kicking, wailing,
and beating the ground until I was spent. If Dake was around, he'd stand
and watch me from his yard and then say, "Bev? Bev?" There would be no
answer, only screams, cussing, and wailing. "But what's wrong with that
child, eh? Bev, you can do better, you know. Stop cussing like that. What's
wrong with you now?"

I'd tell him, tearfully, that I had no firewood. He'd search his yard and
bring me some, saying something like, "Bev, there's no problem so hard
that it can't be fixed. Just try and have some patience."

But that day Dake wasn't around to help me out. "I'm going to kick this darn pot off the fire!" I screamed, cursing. I lifted my right foot to do so, and while it was in mid-air, Sweet Breeze called out, "Don't kick the pot off the fire! You're too miserable!" Then after a short pause, he continued. "I know just what you need."

With that, I felt what seemed like a splash of sparkling cold water all over my body, as if someone had poured a huge bucket of cool spring water over my head and it was running down my body to my feet. It was so cool and refreshing, and the whole situation was so funny that I burst into uncontrollable laughter. The plan was to kick the pot off the fire and then have a good roll in the dirt and scream and wail until I had no strength left, then I'd get up, looking as if I was clothed in sackcloth and ashes, and yell at God, "See what happens to people when you refuse to know them?" That definitely did not happen that day.

I was in a much better mood, so Sweet Breeze said, "Come on, let's go find some firewood so you can finish cooking." I walked off into the bushes with Sweet Breeze in search of firewood. On the way, Sweet Breeze said, "One day you're going to look back on all of this and laugh." Then, after a long pause, he added, "You're going to be a _____ person." (I choose to leave that blank until it comes to pass.)

Without realizing what I was saying, I responded, "I know, God, I believe I'm going to be a _____ person one day. I'm going to work very hard to leave this miserable life behind. But I will never ever tell anyone how poor I was, because my poverty is worse than any _____ person I've ever heard or read about." I gathered the firewood and finished cooking dinner and then ran off to join the marble game, totally forgetting about that conversation with Sweet Breeze until I was in the process of writing this book.

CHAPTER FIVE

Jesus, Up Close and Personal: The Worst Bible Story Ever

I no sooner found a way to deal with the problem of God and the Holy Spirit when I encountered a major problem with Jesus. It was around the Easter holidays. I was about six or seven years old, give or take a year or two. I remember us kids being excited that we were going to see a movie about Jesus at church; it wasn't often that we got to see a movie at church. I'd seen *Samson and Delilah, David*, cowboy movies, Greek mythology movies, and so forth at Count C's movie-theatre-bar-grocery-shop-dance-hall, which was only a two-minute walk down the road and across the street from Top Yard. But we had to pay or sneak our way into Count C's place. So we were thrilled to learn that we'd be watching not just one but two free movies at church.

The movie night arrived. I took my seat in the second or third row, because others had beaten me to the front seats. The first movie was about the villainous captain of a ship who got tired of his evil ways and gave his life to God. The feature movie started, and by the time Jesus and his disciples set off for Jerusalem, I was no longer sitting on the pew in church watching the movie unfold. I had set off walking briskly with Jesus and his disciples because I could sense that something big was about to happen in Jerusalem. From the way Jesus conducted himself until then, I had no reason to expect anything less than a spectacular showdown. He and his men looked purposeful, like men on a mission of the utmost importance, like *The Magnificent Seven*, only more important, because Jesus could do miraculous things.

There was going to be a big showdown in Jerusalem. The Roman soldiers came to escort Jesus off to Pilate's hall. I was a little perturbed that Jesus didn't start fighting back right there and then, but I thought to myself, *Perhaps he's just more or less building them up to knock them down later.* I sometimes did that at school when a bully challenged me. I'd go all out with my dramatic fighting technique—building him up so I could spring my surprise attack on him. I'd start crying, "I'm going to tell my mother. I'm going to tell my mother. I'm going to tell my mother on you when I get home. You wait and see. You wait and see." Thinking I was a crybaby, the bully would get all big and bad. Laughing with confidence, he'd hit me even more to show off before the schoolmates looking on. And that's when I'd pounce on him, catching him off guard, and turn the tables while the crowd laughed at the look of shock on his face.

When the soldiers began beating and spitting on Jesus, Sister Gloria Jackson and others, including children such as Sharon Tyndale, started sniffling and crying, feeling sorry for Jesus. I didn't feel sorry for Jesus. I was getting angry with him. I kept telling him to fight back. I shouted, "Jesus, I know you're going to die, but at least take Pilate down with you. Give the people something to remember you by."

Through her tears, Sharon Tyndale, sitting in front of me, turned to me and said, "He's not going to fight back. he's never going to fight back. He's the one who said if someone hits you, you should turn the other cheek."

I was aghast. "What? 'Turn the other cheek?' *Turn the other cheek?*" My voice carried more than a hint of scorn at such a suggestion.

"Yes, turn the other cheek. It's the new way," Sharon explained.

"The new way?"

"Yes, the new way. It takes more strength not to hit someone back when they hit you than it does to hit them back. That's why Jesus says to turn the other cheek."

I turned away from her in anger and contempt, mumbling to myself that I liked the old way better, because I didn't plan on taking licks from anyone. When I saw Jesus hanging on the cross, I felt no pity for him. I asked him if he was sure he wasn't just a coward hiding behind the fancy talk of turning the other cheek. "What kind of a Bible person is this? And what kind of Bible story is this?" I wondered aloud. "That's not how the Bible goes. That's not how the *Bible* goes. You're post (supposed) to fight back. You're post to fight back," I pointed out to Jesus in anger. I tried to watch the movie some more, but I just could not take in any more. I had reached my limit. Throwing my hands up over my head in exasperation. I yelled, "Oh, Lord, He's messing up the Bible. He's *messing up* the Bible. He's *messing up the whole Bible.* He's not my hero, and I'm not watching any more of this spectacle! Bible people don't go out like this. We go down fighting."

I stopped following the story as it unfolded on the screen. One eye looked away, wanting nothing to do with Jesus, but the other eye still stared accusingly at Jesus, hoping he'd come to his senses, get down off that cross, and do something. I was hoping he'd take the cross and beat the crowd the way Samson beat the Philistines with the jawbone of an ass. Or, if he wanted to be cool and not get all sweaty, just melt the Roman soldiers' swords and make me laugh. I imagined the Roman soldiers dropping their melting swords and running home to their mothers, asking them to beg Jesus to spare them. They were a bunch of cowards without their swords.

But Jesus did neither. Instead, he said, "Father, forgive them, for they know not what they do."

"What? I think they darn well knew what they were doing, and if it was me hanging on that cross, I'd say, 'Father, forgive me for what I am about to do.' Then I would come down off the cross, part the crowd with my cross, and beat up everybody—with God's help, of course."

By the time they took Jesus down, I was livid, fuming at him for letting Bible people down in such a disgraceful manner. Resurrection morning came, and I followed the women to the tomb in pretty much the same angry mood. Jesus's victory over death and the grave was all lost on me because he didn't fight back. When Jesus told the women to tell his disciples to meet him in Galilee, I thought, *he has a lot of nerve to show his face anywhere after the spectacle he pulled at Calvary.*

Sulking all the way, I followed slowly at a distance behind Jesus on the road to Emmaus. I sprung back to life when one of the two men said, "Did not our heart burn within us while he was speaking with us?" By now, my heart was not only burning within me, but it was also fuming, steaming, seething, and boiling over. Finally, someone agreed with me. I thought they were saying how angry they were with him for the way he handled himself from Pilate's hall to Calvary. I was getting ready to join their conversation, because my heart was burning with anger too. However, I was forced to abandon siding with them, as it turned out that they were on Jesus's side. They were impressed by his words and resurrection. I was on my own—again.

When Jesus ascended to heaven, I was still mad and not at all impressed by anything he'd done since standing in Pilate's hall. I felt that he'd left an unfinished Bible story down here that he needed to correct according to Bible-story standards. Jesus caused our side to lose badly. If he didn't want to kill anyone, that was okay. He didn't have to kill anyone—just beat them up or melt their swords.

As I watched him ascend, I asked, "God, do you approve of Jesus's Bible story?" I just knew God wouldn't approve. When Jesus got to heaven, God was going to send him back down to do his Bible story over, because it was incomplete. We didn't go out like that. We went out in style. We went down fighting to the very end.

If angels had appeared and asked, "Ye child from Content, why stand ye gazing up to Heaven?" I would have replied, "I'm waiting for God to send Jesus back down to do his Bible story over, because he didn't do it right."

I went home angry with Jesus and feeling sorry for Judas. Judas hanged himself when he realized what he'd done. Jesus, on the other hand, didn't seem to get that he hadn't done anything to be proud of. He didn't seem to have any regrets about how he handled himself at Calvary.

Usually after seeing a cowboy movie or a Bible story movie, such as *Samson and Delilah* or *David*, my siblings, cousins, and friends—our little gang—would discuss the movie first thing before playing in the morning at Top Yard. Then we'd act it out, shaking "pillars" and slaying everybody with the "jawbone of an ass," or sword fighting, shooting, and dodging bullets. But the morning after the Easter movie, no one mentioned Jesus's movie, let alone acted out any scene from it. No one knew what to make of it. I guess we were all too ashamed and embarrassed about the way it ended to talk about it.

We were well aware that he was going to die. On Good Friday across Jamaica, it was traditional not to cook until well into the afternoon, when it was believed that Jesus had been taken off the cross. Instead, we had fancy, sweet, spicy buns with cheese for breakfast and lunch. As Easter drew near, the grocery shops and supermarkets were filled with these buns. As kids, we looked forward to this time when we could eat bun and cheese for breakfast and lunch. So it wasn't his death that shocked us. It was the way it all went down. We didn't know he'd gone out like that. We'd never seen a hero who didn't fight back, so we didn't experience a feeling of catharsis.

As I was playing at Top Yard that day, Sweet Breeze kept asking me about the movie. Each time he brought up the subject, I yelled, "I don't want to talk about it! I don't want to talk about it!" I walked away and all over the yard, even through the bushes, flourishing my hands and singing loudly to shut out Sweet Breeze and his questioning:

My soul in sad exile was out on life's sea,
So burdened with sin, and distressed,
Till I heard a sweet voice
saying, "Make Me your choice,"
And I entered the Haven of Rest.

I've anchored my soul in the haven of rest,
I'll sail the wide seas no more;
The tempest may sweep
o'er the wild stormy deep
In Jesus I'm safe evermore.

Oh, come to the Savior,
He patiently waits
To save by His power divine;

Come, anchor your soul in the haven of rest
And say, "My Beloved is mine."[6]

This song was from the movie that preceded Jesus's Bible story. The lyrics were written on the screen so the audience could sing along. I added the new words "haven" and "exile" to my collection. I loved the lyrics of this song, so I went home and learned them from a hymn book that I had borrowed from church. I was particularly impressed with the end of the movie when the sailor, the subject of the song, stood on the deck of his ship singing this song loudly and flourishing his hands as the rain poured down on him and the wind tossed his ship to and fro. So I went about the yard dancing and flourishing my hands like the captain, singing loudly, hoping to drown out Sweet Breeze's voice.

But in the midst of my song and flourish, Sweet Breeze kept asking me to discuss the movie. I shouted again and again, "I don't want to talk about it!" Then I walked off muttering angrily, "I don't want to talk about it. I've never been so embarrassed in my whole life. That's the worst Bible story I've ever heard. Wait a minute, I'm not finished. That's got to be the worst Bible story ever."

Sweet Breeze asked the question again. "What do you think about Jesus's Bible story?"

I responded abruptly. "What Bible story? What Bible story? There is no story. He went up to Jerusalem. He let them beat him up. That's it. End of story. I like the other movie better." I continued to walk all over the yard, mumbling, "He could've done better. He could've done better. If God was on his side, he could've done better. He let them beat Him up. He let them kill him. That he died isn't the worst part. It's the way he went out that's bothering me. He didn't go out in style like Samson. He didn't fight like David. Saul has slain his thousands, David his ten thousands. Jesus, zero. What kind of Bible story is that?"

Sweet Breeze asked, "Was it all that bad? Isn't there any part of the story that you like?"

After some thought, I replied, "I only liked the part where Jesus was praying in the Garden of Gethsemane. And that's it."

Time passed, and my anger toward Jesus and his turn-the-other-cheek philosophy cooled somewhat. I called Jesus up close to discuss what he intended to prove by this new turn-the-other-cheek attitude. "Jesus," I said, "You know how I love to read my books quietly, by myself. Are you saying that if I'm sitting down under a tree quietly reading and someone comes up to me and slaps my face for no reason, I should turn my other cheek so he can slap me again? Why, that's like going to Samuel to inquire whether Israel should go and fight the Philistines, and Samuel saying go but be sure to remember to be nice and turn the other cheek. I can just hear the roar of laughter in the camp of the Philistines when they hear of our new fighting strategy."

I decided I was never going to turn the other cheek. Moses fought back. David fought back. Samson fought back. Even Abraham fought back, and God didn't hold it against them. So I was going to fight back too. One didn't have to be overly good to please God. Look at Abraham, for instance. I could hardly picture him as a fighter. I saw him more as a gentle, peaceful person. He gave up the better part of the land to Lot to avoid a confrontation between Lot's shepherds and *his* shepherds. Yet when push came to shove, he went down to Chedorlaomer and fought and brought Lot and his possessions back home.

I told Jesus that I didn't understand this new way of fighting he was talking about. "Jesus," I said, "I know why you can afford to talk like this. It's because you didn't attend York Town Primary School. If you did, you would've changed your mind. The kids you grew up with in Israel were probably all good kids who went to church and didn't fight."

The verse of scripture most quoted by the children of York Town Primary was Exodus 21:24, where Moses said, *"eye for eye, tooth for tooth,"* or as they so eloquently put it, "Yigh fi yigh and teet fi teet." If I were to turn the other cheek, they'd pick on me every day at school. In fact, they'd beat the heck out of *anyone* who believed in turning the other cheek.

There were days when the kids at my school would walk into class saying something like, "D'you know what I had for dinner last night? Mama made some cornmeal dumplings. Cornmeal dumplings make a man strong. I can feel them dumplings moving up in my body, giving me too much energy. I need to work it off." Then they'd start jumping around, flexing muscles, and imitating Muhammad Ali. If no teacher was present, they'd grab the nearest kid and begin to "work it off"—play fighting— which sometimes didn't end always end in smiles and laughter. Sometimes at recess and on the way home, there would be arguments and disagreements of various sizes and for various reasons. Even some of the Christian kids were tempted to temporarily "put down the Bible and fight" and then take it up again, because they were sick and tired of being picked on.

I determined that I wasn't going to take any punches from anyone. I said, "Jesus, I can't just do the turn-the-other-cheek thing. In fact, I'm going in the opposite direction. Whenever someone hits me once, I'm going to hit them back three times—once to return the slap, the other for disturbing my peace, and the third a kick or hard slap to remind him or her to think twice before hitting me again." The teachers at York Town Primary nicknamed me "young warrior" or "little warrior" and snickered behind their sleeves whenever I beat up bullies bigger than I was. They simply said, "I know Beverley didn't start this fight" and let it go at that. I was the self-styled gentle rebel. My motto was, "I start no war, but I end them all."

Only Mr. Polson had a problem with my fighting. One day our teacher was absent, so Mr. Polson was manning both his and her class when I got into a fight with a boy. Mr. Polson saw us out of the corner of his eye and came running over and punished the boy for fighting a girl. He then went back to his desk and sat there scratching his head. Something inside me said, *Run to the bathroom. He's in shock. He's coming back for you as soon as it sinks in.* But I didn't run. He came back and punished me for fighting, asking me, much to the class's amusement, "Are you a girl or a boy?" Mr. Polson was new and not used to my fighting skills. Once I jumped on top of the desk and jumped on the boy and duked it out with him like I saw Tarzan and the cowboys do in the movies.

I had a long talk with Jesus. Actually, it was more of a long statement of my position on the turn-the-other-cheek method. "Jesus," I said, "me naw falla you. Me naw falla you (I am not following you). Nobody is going to beat me up the way they beat you up at Calvary. I used to think like you once. Yvonne used to pick on me and my brother and sister every day. I wouldn't fight back, because I was a coward, afraid of her big mouth, but also because I simply had no desire to fight anyone. Until one day when Yvonne dragged me about the yard with her teeth sunk into my skin, beating the heck out of me. We were both in our underwear because of the heat. I cried out for help. 'Nobody help her,' the adults commanded. 'She was born before Yvonne. She has to learn to defend herself. What's going to happen to her when she starts school?' The whole yard, including the adults, gathered to watch the spectacle.

"Yvonne loves an audience, loves to put on a show. She dragged me toward Ya Ya's old bed under the tree to finish me off, but being called worthless stung me really hard. That day I became a fighter. I grabbed Yvonne with a hot-fire vengeance, and although I can't recall exactly what happened next, my retaliation was such that Yvonne never dared to pick a fight with me again. Yvonne and I became the best of friends after that, holding hands all the way to Denbigh Junior Secondary School and beyond. She bullied every kid in the yard and even at school, except me.

"Throughout the years, the kids in the yard, when bullied by her, would ask her, 'You pick on everybody. Why don't you pick on Bev, huh?' Yvonne never answered. So, Jesus," I said, "me naw falla you in turning the other cheek. It doesn't work around York Town Primary kids. And by the way, you didn't need to think about calling down ten thousand angels to set you free at Calvary. One angel standing by your cross would've done the trick, because all of them Roman soldiers were a bunch of cowards. If they had seen one angel standing by you, they would've thrown their swords down and run to their mothers' houses, begging them to pray to God to take his angel away."

As if to contradict my own motto, I ended many a war in victory at home and at York Town Primary, only to end up crying, "God, this doesn't feel good. My whole day is ruined. I don't like fighting, but they won't leave me alone, and I can't bear the shame associated with getting beaten up. But I can't turn the other cheek."

I subconsciously parted company with Jesus and the movie that led up to my discussion with him, but even as I made my rebellious statement,

I still remembered the day I invited Jesus into my heart. Sometime prior to the movie, the pastor, or perhaps it was my Sunday school teacher, had made the recommendation after we had sung, "Into my heart, into my heart, come into my heart, Lord Jesus. Come into my heart today, come and stay. Come into my heart, Lord Jesus."[7]

I had asked, "Why do I need to invite Jesus into my heart?" And I was told that He would help me keep my heart clean for God. It sounded like a good deal, so I invited Jesus in and watched him shrink himself to fit inside my heart. He didn't seem too comfortable, because my heart was too tiny and was enclosed within my chest. He was standing on one leg because there wasn't enough room there for him to stand on both feet. It seemed as if Jesus was imprisoned in my heart, and I wondered why he wouldn't rather stay with me on the outside in the sunshine where we could have more fun walking and talking to each other.

I didn't un-invite Jesus from my heart after the movie and the subsequent discussion with him. Rather, I just refused to think about or speak to him. I avoided any conversations about Jesus and simply referred to him in my thoughts as the turn-the-other-cheek person.

One Sunday afternoon, Pastor, as a preface to ending the altar call and concluding the day's service, quoted the song that went as follows:

> *Jesus is standing in Pilate's hall—*
> *Friendless, forsaken, betrayed by all...*
> *What will you do with Jesus?*
> *What will you do with Jesus?*
> *Neutral you cannot be;*
> *Someday your heart will be asking,*
> *"What will He do with me?"*[8]

The words "neutral you cannot be" leaped out at me, but I stared past Pastor, through the walls of the church, looking firmly ahead, unmoved. I was following in the footsteps of my hero, Bible David. I was a fighter. I was hanging out on the rocks of En Gedi with David. I wasn't going to join the turn-the-other-cheek army. I left Jesus in a neutral position in my heart. I was not against him, but I was most certainly not in favour of turning the other cheek or dying on the cross for anyone.

But let me provide some pertinent details that long preceded my eventual refusal to adhere to the turn-the-other-cheek way of living. One Sunday as Pastor Eddie got ready to preach the sermon, he held up a book and said something about it being the Bible. I looked at the book long and hard. That was the first time I became aware that the Bible was indeed a book, not just a series of stories in Sister Betty's shoe boxes. I said under my breath, "The Bible people wrote a book? Sister Betty didn't tell me that."

I got hold of a Bible as soon as I could, just before the evening service commenced. I grabbed it from one of the pews and ran with it to a quiet corner. I began turning the pages in earnest, swiftly but carefully, moving my fingers across each word, each line, becoming ever more anxious with the turn of each new page. Sweet Breeze asked, "What are you looking for?" I ignored him and continued my search, feeling dejected and rejected with each turn of the page. I looked the very picture of sadness. Sweet Breeze repeated the question.

I placed my finger on the page so I wouldn't lose my place. "Shh, I can't stop to talk with you right now. You're interrupting me. You're going to make me lose my place." Then I ignored Sweet Breeze and returned to the book. I was becoming more desperate as I turned each page and found no sign of what I was searching for. And once again, Sweet Breeze broke into my concentration, "What are you looking for?"

"I'm looking for my name. I'm looking for my name." My frantic search continued, and I grew increasingly alarmed as I moved closer to the end of the book. Then I came upon a word close to my name: "Verily, verily." It was repeated twice and sounded almost like Beverley. Maybe the Bible people didn't hear my name right. After all, they had heard it from afar, and it was a new name for them. It was okay if they didn't get it right, as long as they didn't forget to mention me. I read on, but what followed didn't suggest that it was a message addressed directly to me.

That day I searched the Bible from Genesis to Revelation and found no mention of my name. At the end of my seeking, I sat on the verge of tears, the most pitiful look on my face, staring in disbelief at the book my friends had written.

My shoulders slumped. My mind reeled. *I don't believe this*, I thought. *I can't believe they left me out of their book. They never mentioned my name. They never mentioned my name! They didn't leave me anything. Abraham, you didn't leave anything for me? How could you do this to me? Moses, how could you forget to leave something for me? I can't believe you all didn't see me coming. And David, of all the people in the Bible, I can't believe that you left me out.*

"What were you hoping to find?" Sweet Breeze asked.

"I was hoping the Bible people would say something about me. I was especially hoping David would tell me, 'Bev, when thou art come (born and grown up), go to Israel and search by the rocks and bushes at En Gedi, and there find a sandal I left for you.'"

I had seen a picture of David by the rocks at En Gedi, hiding from King Saul, wearing a nice pair of leather sandals. The Bible says, "Thou shalt not covet," but I coveted those sandals; they looked so good. I wanted David to leave me one of his sandals and keep the other, because I didn't want him to give me something he didn't want or no longer needed. I wanted him to loan me his favourite sandal because he loved it and chose to pass it on to me to keep here on Earth and return to him when I saw him in heaven.

Sweet Breeze sighed, as if wondering why all this fuss about one sandal. His reaction caused me to think about my expectation. Suddenly, I laughed loudly and said, "That's a silly idea, isn't it? Well, I don't like jewellery that much. I only like earrings, and I don't think David wore earrings. Then again, maybe he did, because I've seen pictures of pirates and other warriors with an earring or two in their ears, but those earrings are gaudy. I like small, dainty earrings, and I don't think David wore those. I know it's not polite to ask people for money, jewellery, or gold or silver coins. I just want one of David's sandals."

"So what are you going to do with one sandal?"

"I'm going to put it on my mantelpiece. When people come to my house, they'll ask what I'm doing with such an old, tattered sandal on my mantelpiece in an otherwise immaculate house. And I'll tell them that it's a sandal that belongs to Bible David, and that he left it in his will in the Bible for me. I'll tell them that when my life is over, I'm going to take it to heaven and return it to David, because it's his favourite sandal, and he just wanted me to have it for a while and then bring it back safely to him, because he has the other one."

"Your mantelpiece?"

"Yes, my mantelpiece. Didn't I tell you I'm going away to America? Well, I'm not staying here. I'm going to America when I grow up. And according to what I've learned from books and movies, the houses in America have fireplaces with mantelpieces above them. I love the word mantelpiece, and that's where I intend to keep David's sandal. But none of the Bible people mentioned my name. They should have known I was coming. They should have known I was coming. They're prophets and can see into the future. They should have looked down the road and seen me coming. I'm a Bible person too, but my name isn't in the Bible. And now there's only a tiny space at the end of the Bible, and my story can't fit there. Does this mean I don't belong?"

"The Bible was written a long time ago about people from another time," Sweet Breeze explained. "It had to end so you could have it, but there's a new Bible being written for your time, and you'll be in that one."

"Well, even if I'll be in the new Bible for my time, they should have mentioned me in the old Bible, so that when people see me in the new Bible, they'll know without a doubt that I am a Bible person, that I belong."

The idea of being in the new Bible comforted me for a little while. I could easily picture Billy Graham, a man obviously highly favoured by God, because God allowed him to be born in a place named *Many Apples, Many Soda*, a place, in my mind, similar to the Garden of Eden. I wished I'd been born in a place like that, because I'd be able to eat many apples and drink many sodas all day long.

Then I came to my senses and started whining again.

"But… being in the new Bible isn't the same thing. It's not the same thing," I said to Sweet Breeze. "I don't want to be in the new Bible with a bunch of strangers from my time. I want to be in the old Bible with my old friends Abraham and Moses and David."

Sweet Breeze left me with no answer to my dilemma. I seemed to have exasperated or stumped him with the puzzle of how to fit the new child into the old book with her old friends.

I didn't stay in church much after that God-is-a-Spirit Sunday. Once Sunday school was over, I didn't hang around to hear Pastor Eddie preaching on his favourite subject—spirit. It didn't help Pastor's case either when I noticed that his little daughter, Ruth, had a penchant for twiddling her fingers and talking to the air. I turned to my friend Lillian sitting next to me and asked, "What's Ruthie doing?" Lillian interpreted Ruthie's Down's Syndrome behaviour with the understanding of a child. She replied nonchalantly, "She's talking to fallen angels."

"Fallen angels?"

"Yes, fallen angels," Lillian replied.

"What's a fallen angel?"

"Well, when God kicked the devil and the rebellious angels out of heaven, some of the most powerful ones stayed in the air, and they're called fallen angels. That's who Ruthie is talking to."

I was surprised and shocked at hearing that angels fell from heaven along with the devil, and even more so that Pastor's daughter was communicating with them, in church, in sight of the congregation. This new bit of information left me puzzled and confused about who, or what, spirits were. But I didn't let that hinder my growth or development in Bible knowledge. For my personal Bible study, I read and covered the words "spirit" and "ghost" with my fingertips whenever I came across them. I did the same with the hymn books or wherever and whenever I encountered those words. I got to be a real Bible expert, to the point where I knew to avoid reading certain books of the Bible, especially Daniel and Revelation, because they had monsters in them with lots of heads and eyes. And when I read that Goliath had six fingers, I worried that God's refusing to know me was because I also was born with six fingers and may be related to Goliath.

Although I had pretty much washed my hands of Pastor Eddie, his son David was my Sunday school teacher, and we adored him. Pastor had five sons and four daughters—sometimes Paul wasn't nice, but there was something special about David. He was well-liked by us children, and even the adults, because he was just as pleasant as his namesake in the Bible. David played the guitar and led the children in fun and lively praise and worship during Sunday school. Then we went to our respective classes.

David, my Sunday school teacher for both my primary and junior classes, was also, for a short time, my teacher at Sister Betty's school. In Sunday school, he would teach the day's lesson and our memory verse from the Bible. Close to the end of the hour, he'd give us our workbooks to answer the questions and do the puzzles pertaining to the lesson. I looked forward to this part of the hour, because I didn't like to participate verbally.

While David was going through the lessons, I sometimes went off into space, arguing with God and asking questions such as, "Why did you bother to call King Saul, Samson, and King Solomon? You knew they were going to be failures in the end, so why did you waste time calling them?" I even waxed philosophical, saying stuff like, "If the end justifies the means, and all's well that ends well, why waste your time calling them in the first place? You knew how they were going to end. Their end certainly didn't justify the means whereby you called them. They didn't end well. Why don't you call me? I'd be so faithful."

I asked God this particular question during a lesson on Elijah, and then David called out me. "Bev, you're not paying attention to the lesson—again."

"I am paying attention," I mumbled.

He said, "Okay, what's the name of the brook by which Elijah hid?"

"Cherith." I was good at one-word answers.

He raised an eyebrow in surprise and then asked, "And what tribe did I say Elijah belonged to?"

"Tishbite," I answered.

David sighed. "I don't know how you know the answers, but I know you weren't paying attention."

I smiled on the inside, because my secret was to peek ahead in our workbook to see the following week's lesson. Then I'd go home and read it in the Bible, making mental notes of things that my teacher would likely ask during or at the end of the lesson. I called it my read-and-file system. I pictured Elijah sitting under the cherry tree beside the canal that ran by our church in order to remember him sitting by the brook Cherith. David often took our class under the cherry tree on Sundays when the weather was nice. I simply couldn't forget Elijah's Tishbite tribe because the name was too funny. But I filed it under titty-biter, the name we kids had for tadpoles. The tadpoles were in the canal.

David concluded the lesson by reminding us that God often speaks to us in the still, small voice with which he revealed himself to Elijah. But that information went right over my head. I was still expecting God to show up at my house and call me by name.

David promised to take us on a journey through the entire Bible. He said we didn't know what fate awaited us in the future. We might even be imprisoned for our faith. His intention was to make us into living Bibles so that if they took our Bible away and locked us in prison, we'd have the Word of God hidden in our hearts, because they couldn't take that away. David had a real passion for his biblical namesake and stayed on the life of David for a long time. As he took us through the story of Bible David, we laughed at the funny names. One name, Ahitophel, sounded to us like "I hit—you fell."

Through both Davids, I learned that man looks on the outward appearance, but God looks on the heart (1 Samuel 16:7). This made my heart glad, because all I had going for me on my outward appearance were bones—lots of bones. I also learned that it was possible for a human being to be a person "after God's own heart." David, our teacher, explained that although Bible David wasn't perfect like God, his heart was full of praise, and he was always ready to ask for forgiveness when he did wrong. Our David was so moved by Bible David that he cried hard and long in front of us during our lesson on David, Bathsheba, and Uriah, and we in turn were so moved by this that there wasn't one giggle. Not even from Yvonne. We just sat with bowed heads in a sacred moment, on the verge of tears ourselves, not knowing why we felt like weeping along with him.

Sunday after Sunday, we studied Bible David until we were well-saturated with knowledge about his life. Growing up in sugarcane country, where the land was flat and caves and mountains were far away, I became fascinated with caves and mountains, because they seemed so much more challenging and mysterious. Plus, all of my favourite people had something to do with caves and mountains—God, Moses, Abraham, David, and even our local national heroes, Nanny and the Maroons. In my imagination, I was always hanging out with Bible David by the rocks and caves of En Gedi, roughing it in the wild. I fell in love with the words "En Gedi" and added them to my collection. I didn't know if I added them to my collection because they sounded like the words "en garde," words we captured from sword fighting or fencing in the movies and used whenever we played those games, or simply because of the way they sounded and their connection to Bible David.

During the course of our lessons on Bible David, we fell deeper in love with him. We declared that he was the first person we were going to look for when we got to heaven. He was a shepherd boy who became king. He played his harp and, like us, he loved to sing. He wrote most of the psalms. He killed Goliath. He was a man of valour, a mighty warrior. He had his weak moments, but he also had a heart, as demonstrated by his refusal to kill Saul when he found him in the cave at En Gedi. More importantly, God said David was a man after his own heart.

David was, without doubt, my favourite of the Bible heroes, and I wanted to follow in his footsteps. I had two scrawny, pimply-faced boys to beat up at church. One of them was Pastor's son, Paul, and the other was Sister Myrie's son, John. They kept making fun of me in church, and I wanted to wipe the smirks off their faces.

Case in point, Yvonne and I tried to sing a song one Tuesday night during Christian Endeavour, as our youth meeting was called. It didn't go too well. Guess who couldn't stop giggling? John and Paul, of course. Sister Betty came to our rescue and helped us finish the song. I made a mental note to beat up both boys. And the song we were singing? *"At Calvary."*

Years I spent in vanity and pride,
Caring not my Lord was crucified,
Knowing not it was for me he died
on Calvary.

Mercy there was great and grace was free,
Pardon there was multiplied to me,
There my burdened soul found liberty—
At Calvary

O the love that drew salvation's plan!
O the grace that brought it down to man!
O the mighty gulf that God did span
At Calvary.[9]

I loved the song but paid no attention to the words. I wanted to sing it because I had heard the teenage girls singing it, but it wasn't as easy to sing as I thought.

Another night, I had my sister's or my brother's sleeping head on my lap. I sort of rested my head on him or her. When I held up my head, a tiny pool of drool trickled out and I wiped it away quickly. But not before John saw it and commented to Paul, "Do you think we got about a quart or bucketful there?" Oh boy, was I ever going to get them for that.

Then one Sunday morning I arrived at Sunday school late. I was going to help my cousin Judith get ready for Sunday school and wanted to get there before they started singing the lively children's action songs. I got to church and discovered the children had finished singing and were now in their respective classes. I hated missing the action songs we sang during Sunday school praise and worship. To make matters worse, I walked into church, where my Sunday school class was being held that day along with two other classes, adult and intermediate, and was accosted by Pastor Eddie, who accused me of running around in church with the other children before Sunday school. I tried to explain that I had just gotten there. As I did, I heard John and Paul giggling in their class, the teenage class, which was perpendicular to mine inside the church. I thought, *They think this is funny? Wait till I get my hands on them. I'll show them funny.*

But I had several problems in my way to beating them up. My first was how to corner them separately, or even together, in the right time and place, because I didn't want Pastor or David to see me fighting. Another was that neither of the boys lived close to me or attended my school, so I'd have to hit them at church, and preferably when there were no adults around. In addition, I didn't want word to get back to Pastor or David. I wanted to avoid being interrogated by them about whether any of the Bible lessons were getting through to me, because they'd spoken about Jesus's teaching on turning the other cheek and God bringing peace on Earth, goodwill to all, and so forth.

My main problem was that I didn't know if God would hold it against me for beating up Paul. Bible David didn't hurt King Saul, because King Saul was still God's anointed. I didn't know if Pastor Eddie was God's anointed, because he spoke too much about spirit. And if Pastor was indeed God's anointed, was that anointing passed on to his son Paul? I didn't think so, but I was reluctant to run the risk of not following David's example and, thereby, offending God.

The problem resolved itself. I noticed that John had been missing from church for some time. When I inquired, I learned that he and his family had migrated to Canada. I counted him a lucky boy and left it at that. Paul kind of lost his uppity grin after John left, so there was no point pursuing him to wipe off a smirk that was no longer there. But I still had some boys at school to beat up. Boys were now my number one enemy. I stuck to more immediate problems, such as how to shut the boys up at York Town Primary from referring to me as "The Human Skeleton"—the title seen above pictures of the human body used in class to teach students about its various parts and their functions.

By the time I started York Town Primary School, I had somewhat given up any hope of God coming to my house, and I stopped waiting for him to show up at my gate. In fact, from the Sunday afternoon Pastor mentioned that God was a spirit, I stopped running to the gate to look for God. I consoled myself by saying, "God, if you're not in the Bible story business anymore, you can still come and visit me. Come visit me and call me by my name, the way you called Moses and Abraham, and make me happy." I still expected God to let me know that he knew me, but I didn't really expect him to come down the lane to my house. Yet I don't think I wanted God to call me in the night either, the way he called Samuel, because then the conversation would have been:

"Bev!"

"Who's calling me?"

"It's me."

"Me who?"

"God. You called me to come to your house. Do you remember?"

"Where are you?"

"I'm right here."

"Where? I can't see you. Uh-huh. Are you wearing flesh or are you wearing spirit?"

Then I'd grab my blanket and wrap myself from head to toe, teeth chattering, bones shaking, and ask God to go away because I couldn't, and wouldn't, speak to no spirit God.

So I left Jesus' to camp with Bible David on the rocks of En Gedi because I love the words En Gedi and also because I like the idea of roughing it in caves and on mountains.

CHAPTER SIX

Author! Author!

Life at York Town Primary School was idyllic, pastoral, and picture perfect, except for two major problems: the boys who continued calling me skinny in as many different words from both the English and Jamaican thesauruses *and* the teachers who kept telling me to pursue writing as a career.

"Garling, garling, gunner man ah come (is coming). Pow! Pow! Pow! Pow!" The boys took aim and fired at all the skinny girls in shorts, but especially at me, during sports day or outdoor physical education. Garlings are long-legged white birds that followed cattle around, picking insects off their bodies. The boys applied this chant to the skinny girls at school, especially during track and field team meet when everyone had to wear shorts.

One morning I got ready for a track and field meet in my team-coloured shorts, feeling very athletic and ready to win a few for my team. I walked over to my team with an angry look on my face because the boys were teasing me, yet again, about my skinny legs. They sat on the sidelines yelling, "Garling, garling, chicken legs, mosquito legs, bird legs." They laid in wait for skinny girls, and their yells grew louder as I walked by in my shorts. I wanted to go over and beat them to a pulp.

"Your mother!" I shouted back. I wanted to punch them and wipe the silly grins off their faces.

"Don't let them get to you. Just ignore them," Lillian implored. "Don't let them know they're getting to you. It will only make them tease you more," she advised.

I walked over to my team feeling everything but enthusiastic. "C'mon, Bev, get some team spirit!" Elsa, my team captain, shouted, trying to get me revved up for the games. I was one of her best track and field runners, but I didn't look like I was going to win anything with that look on my face. And then there was that word "spirit" again. It was one thing to try to put the boys out of my mind and concentrate on the race, but I was sure not going to get into any spirit to do so. I didn't do too badly that day, but I didn't get into any spirit.

I was not only mad because the boys were teasing me. I was also mad because I'd been praying to God to help me gain some weight, and He didn't seem to be answering my prayer. When I gained some weight, it would prove that God knew me. It would also put an end to the boys' teasing. Even my brother joined in, grinning at my lack of flesh. While teaching us about Joseph's interpretation of Pharaoh's dream about the seven fat and seven lean kine, I heard Glen quietly snickering in the pew behind me. Without looking back, I knew he was grinning because he had just learned a new name to call me. Glen whispered, "Bev, David says seven *lean* kines. Lean. You get it? Lean."

"He said seven fat ones too," I retorted.

At first, I thought God would hear my prayer and just click his fingernails together and say, "Bev, get fat," just as he had said, "Let there be light," and there was light. I prayed hard each night, tears streaming down my face, telling God I couldn't take being called all kinds of names anymore. I asked him to let me stop growing lengthwise, then I'd curl up in bed so that I'd grow width-wise.

I dreamed of, and hoped for, the morning when I took my uniform off on the playground to reveal legs with some meat on them in my shorts. The boys would open their mouths to chant their annoying chants and keel right over when they saw my new legs. Oh, how I anticipated that day. But after waking up quite a few mornings looking for flesh on my bones and not finding any, I consoled myself that God was going to make me gain weight slowly over time. Each morning I convinced myself that I had gained a pound or two. But then, at the track and field games or during physical education outdoors, the boys' chants said I was still very much skinny. That caused me to doubt God and lose the weight I believed I had gained in my sleep. I wanted to beat them up and make them shut up so that the weight would stay.

Everyone seemed to think I was too tall and skinny for my age. Some said I was going to be over seven feet tall when I grew up, and others said I was going to be longer than my bed and taller than my husband. I didn't want to grow anymore. My kind of skinny was not in. I wanted to gain some weight.

Meanwhile, even as I bemoaned my fate as a tall, skinny girl, my teachers had noticed my love of reading, spelling, and writing, and were constantly asking me what I wanted to be when I grew up. They all thought I should go into writing. I, on the other hand, believed I should become involved in something to do with children. I hated this stinking world and didn't want anything to do with it, except making unwanted children happy. I made up my mind that when I grew up, I was going to build a big, white house with red windowsills and a high fence to keep adults out. I planned on borrowing Dake's dray cart to go about asking for unloved children and taking them there to live with me. I was going to place flowers on the windowsill and plant flowers and trees in the yard and install a big bird bath to encourage birds and butterflies to come and stay with us. I didn't fancy cooking or any type of housework, so I still had some details to work out, but I would ensure that the kids had Cornflakes and bread for breakfast. That was easy to make. And when the delivery men came by with bread and other items, they'd have to leave their deliveries outside the gate, because no adults were allowed inside.

My mother began to increase my share of the housework, and that helped cement my decision to not stick around and let her make a domestic fowl out of me. I was going to become a migratory bird and fly away to America to become a cowboy. We were learning about domestic and migratory birds, and I drew a parallel between the lesson and my situation at home. Domestic birds stayed home, while migratory birds flew over land and sea. In the movies, cowboys didn't stay home and do housework. They rode for miles, slept under the stars, and for meals used a few utensils that they washed in the river before continuing their ride. I didn't care to shoot anyone. I simply wanted to ride my horse and follow the beautiful rugged mountains, hills, rivers, and desert scenery until I couldn't hear my mother calling me to come do housework anymore. I was going along for the ride, the adventure, the thrill of riding a horse downhill, across the plains, over the mountain, and through the river.

Dale Evans' horse's name was Trigger. I wondered what my horse's name would be. Free Spirit came to mind, but, of course, I didn't use that word. I thought of the name Born Free. It wasn't quite as catchy as I'd like it to be, but it summed up what I and my horse were about—freedom. So it would do. "Born Free, as free as the wind blows, as free as the grass grows, born free to follow [my] heart."[10]

I was lean and lanky like a cowboy, and I could fight like one, so that was obviously what I was supposed to be. I heard the older men in the cowboy movies advising young men to go west and make their fortune. I was a girl, but I was taking their advice and heading west also. I figured they didn't want women out west, and that was precisely why I was going. I not only hated housework, but I also couldn't stand the damsels in distress portrayed in the movies. They were always running from danger and falling down or fainting, waiting to be rescued by a man. I was not like that. I could run from danger without falling, or stand up and fight if I had to. They could use a woman like me out west to put a different spin on things.

I was going out west on a long journey to pan for gold, and when my riding days were over, I'd use the money to buy my house with the fireplace and mantelpiece. I didn't mind sharing the journey out west with a partner so that I'd have someone to talk to. But he'd have to sleep under his own tree at nights. I was scared of snakes and terrified of that awful cry coyotes made, so I needed God to help me get to Hollywood, California, to ride horses and to watch over me at night when I slept so that snakes and coyotes wouldn't harm or scare me.

Before running off to school each morning, I'd pause to listen to the BBC World News headlines on the eight o'clock news from London, England. I would hear about how many U.S. soldiers had been killed in Vietnam, and how many Israeli soldiers had been killed in the Middle East. I shook my head and said, "Something is wrong in Israel. Too many soldiers are dying. They're not reading the news right. The news should have stated that the children of Israel inquired of the Lord if they should go to war." If God wasn't in Israel, where was he?

And what was happening with the men in America, the land of my dreams? At the rate the young men were dying in Vietnam, they'd all be dead by the time I grew up and got there. There wouldn't be any left for me to marry when I was through riding. It didn't seem like God was in America either. Too many soldiers were dying in Vietnam.

One day when my mother was home, she saw the expressions on my face as I listened to the BBC news. "Bev, what does the world news have to do with you?" she asked. "You're a child. Why do you always like to take on such big problems?"

I couldn't tell her that I was searching everywhere for God, and if he wasn't in Israel or America, as gathered from the BBC, then it was possible he was nowhere to be found. The fact that Israel existed, as reported by the BBC, meant that God should exist also, but it appeared no one had heard from him or seen him lately. God was never mentioned in the world news from the BBC. "He's gone up! He's gone up! He's gone up from the whole Earth!" I sighed as I ran off to school.

I got to school, and the teachers started in again about my writing. Although she was never one of my classroom teachers, Mrs. Williams kept asking me to tell my parents to come see her because she wanted to talk to them about a scholarship and so forth. I always told her that I had forgotten to tell them. The truth was I didn't see the point in telling my parents anything, as I wasn't interested in writing. I was interested in a career in riding, and I was only sticking around long enough to get my breasts, and then I'd run away to America. I was tall, but people kept asking for my parents because I was a child. When I got my breasts, they would not ask me "Where's your parent?" when I got to the airport. The scholarship would be better spent on a kid who was planning to stick around. I certainly wasn't going to.

This writing thing all started one morning as Mrs. Broderick passed my desk and saw me writing and liked my penmanship. She stopped to take a closer look at what I was writing and commended me to my new teacher, Miss May. Miss May had a penchant for penmanship and the English language. Cursive writing and grammar were her specialty. She took me under her wing. I was in grade two but should have been in grade one, as this was my first year in school. There were too many kids in grade one, so some of us were sent over to join the grade two class. York Town was a brand-new school with brand-new teachers, and we were still in the process of getting to know each other. I had loved reading and writing since Sister Betty's school, and they just seemed to love me right back.

I spent the first part of the school year at Four Paths Primary. Prior to my starting at Four Paths, Errol said, "Bev, your reading and writing skills are beyond grade one. I think the teachers are going to place you in grade two instead when you start primary school."

"Why?" I asked, all excited. "What do kids do in grade one?"

"Oh, they learn to make the letters of the alphabet properly by printing words, and they do math and stuff like that. But they don't write in cursive until grade two."

"What? More crab toes?" I asked.

"Yup." He smiled.

"I don't want to go through that again. I'm doing cursive writing now."

"Well, you may not have to. When the principal sees how well you can read and write, he's going to send you straight to grade two."

The first day I entered Four Paths Primary, Yvonne's big sister, Bev, or Jislyn as we called her then, took Yvonne and me to the office to be registered. I stood there looking at the principal, expecting him to take one look at me and tell me to go straight to grade two. And when he just took our information, wrote it in his big book, and then told my cousin to take Yvonne and me to grade one, I was in a state of shock. Couldn't he tell that I belonged in grade two? I was not going back to printing crabby crab toes. I wanted to write cursive like an adult.

I got to grade one, took one look at the classroom, and then asked a grade one girl nearby, "Where's grade two?"

"Over there," she replied. And sure enough, there it was, right across the hall.

I ran across the hall and took my seat where I belonged. The teacher and students tried to tell me that I was in the wrong class, but I said, "No, I'm not," and remained firmly in my seat. This situation was causing a great deal of distraction, as the students were laughing about this grade one kid who wanted to be in grade two. "Go to your class," they urged.

"I'm in my class."

We continued this back and forth for some time until the teacher decided to get the principal to settle the matter. He picked me up and took me back to grade one, and I cried, yelled, and screamed, "No, no, no," and ran back to grade two. Now both the grade one and two classes were watching us and snickering. The principal took me back to grade one, and I ran back to grade two, over and over, until I was exhausted. The principal was also exhausted. He eventually relented and told the grade two teacher to give me some work. He said that if I could do the work, I could stay. He said he would come back to check my work.

I was doing the writing part of the test when a girl I knew from Content, who was in grade two and with whom I was sharing a desk, offered to do the math for me. I didn't like math, so I let her do it while I wrote. Later, the principal came to check my work. I passed the writing, but the math was pitiful. What was I thinking when I let her do my math? *Jeez, I could've done way better than that.* The principal said I had to go to grade one because I couldn't do grade two math. I cried, yelled, and screamed again, but I knew I was defeated, because I couldn't tell him the grade two girl had done the math for me. I would have done much better had I done it myself.

The grade one teachers, Miss Scarlet and Miss Stewart, welcomed me with open arms and lots of empathy. "Why don't you like us?" they asked. "You want to be with your big sister in grade two, is that it?"

I was the eldest child in my family. I didn't have a big sister or brother. I just wanted to go to grade two to write like grownups did. I'd been writing long before I entered Sister Betty's school. I used to make horizontal loops and vertical zigzags and refer to them as *reely reely* and *ziggy ziggy* writing. I'd write on my mother's furniture and even on her bedsheets. I'd be totally engrossed in writing, stopping only to look out the door and up into the sky, as if taking dictation from the air, only to feel a sharp slap from my mother, followed by, "Are you crazy? My sheet? You're writing on my *sheet?* Give me that pen."

From then on, pens were kept high and out of reach from me, but I still managed to climb up and get them. I was irresistibly drawn to the pen. After many a slap, I took my writing outdoors and wrote on the ground with bits of sticks.

Cursive writing made me feel free, as if I were untying knots in my stomach. I got more relaxed as the words flowed in cursive from my pen or pencil onto the paper. Cursive writing looked an awful lot like *reely reely* and *ziggy ziggy* writing, only it made more sense. But I couldn't tell Miss Scarlett and Miss Stewart that I wanted to stay in grade two because I wanted to write in cursive.

Unlike the grade one teachers, the grades one and two kids were less forgiving. They wouldn't let me forget that I was the girl who wanted to start school in grade two. I was overjoyed when one morning on our way to Four Paths Primary we heard that the new school at York Town, which was closer to Content, was now accepting students. It was "Bye-bye, Four Paths Primary" and "Hello, York Town Primary."

I was quite settled and very happy in grade one at York Town Primary and had given up starting school in grade two, when I ended up in Miss May's grade two class. Grade one had too many students, and the brighter grade ones were sent to join the grade twos. Miss May, who had a penchant for penmanship and the English language, showed my writing to Mrs. Williams, who in turn showed it to Ms. MacLean, who said, "I don't think she's the real author of her writing. She may be holding the pen, but she's not the real author. I think she's a medium (she whispered that word), and I'll prove it to all of you." Ms. MacLean wrote some incorrect sentences on the blackboard and asked me if they were correct.

"No," I said.

She asked me to correct what was wrong with them, and I did. And then she asked me, "How do you know they were incorrect?"

"Because they don't sound right when I read them."

Then she pointed to a big word and asked me to give her the meaning of the word, which I did. Not yet satisfied, she asked if I'd ever seen the word before.

"No."

My answer somehow satisfied what she hoped to prove, but she gave me another word, and I did the same.

She turned to the teachers and said, "I told you she's not the real author. She's writing by air. A spirit is writing through her. She's a medium." This time she whispered both "medium" and "spirit." They also bandied the word "genius" around, and Ms. Maclean reminded them of the root word from which genius came.

I overhead Mrs. Williams reply, "Well, it's not an evil spirit." And she too whispered the last word.

Mrs. McLean whispered back, "I never said it was an evil spirit. I said she's not the real author, and I have proved my point."

My formula for writing was to sound out the word or sentence first in my head, and something would tell me if the meaning or sense was correct or not. The same went for spelling. I would sound and spell the word in my mind, and something would tell me if it was correct.

One day I was sounding out a word in class to write it, but the children were making too much noise and I couldn't hear myself think. I went outside and wrote the word in the air. Sweet Breeze said, "That's wrong."

I stomped my feet. "What do you mean it's wrong?"

I wrote the word differently, and Sweet Breeze said, "That's correct." I made a funny face at the sky and ran back to class, smiling.

Perhaps a year or two later, another teacher showed my writing to the other teachers, including Mrs. Williams, who called me to her class and said, "Your writing is seasoned. It sounds very familiar. I think I know who you are." She was about to tell me who I was, and I waited anxiously to hear, when she suddenly said, "It's slipped from my memory. It was right on the tip of my tongue and now it's gone." She paused for a while and then said, "I can't wait for you to grow up so I can find out who you are. Please remember me and my words when you do."

Mrs. Williams' husband was a pastor, and she was a very godly person. I guessed later, much later, that she sensed, or rather discerned, that my writing was beginning to sound like a Bible person's.

"Beverly," she asked one day when we were in the hallway, "is someone telling you not to say anything to us about your plans for the future?"

"No," I replied. But I had stood on tiptoes and peered into the future, trying on the various uniforms of the high schools, and I didn't see myself in any of them. What I saw instead was a scene of myself as an adult seated around a table with a group of men.

At York Town Primary, the teachers would sometimes take us out under a tree to teach us a Bible story. Although my school and church weren't affiliated with each other in any way, the lesson would often be the same, and I'd think to myself, *What a coincidence.*

One afternoon as my teacher read us a Bible story under a tree (the same tree from which I would start running from God later), it dawned on me that Bible people's lives were really hard and full of struggles. I wanted a carefree life. I shouted out in my mind, *Thank God that God doesn't know me. I don't want God to know me anymore. I don't want him to call on me. I don't want to be a Bible person anymore.* My shout came back from the air above and flopped on my head just like an unskilled baker's tossed dough. I didn't like the feeling at all. It was the same sinking feeling I got when Sweet Breeze refused to commit to a yes-or-no answer.

One morning just after recess, there was flurry and fluster all over the school about what we wanted to be when we grew up. Most of the children were able write about and even say aloud what they wanted to be. I could not, because I had initially wanted to be the mother of an orphanage but had changed my mind to wanting to be a cowboy. A list of career choices was placed on a blackboard to help students decide. I looked up and down the list and couldn't find my place, as the careers that appealed to me weren't there. At that time, I still wanted my orphanage, but I thought I would die of housework before I finished school. Moreover, I now realized I would need lots of money to build the orphanage and feed the children. In addition, I heard some stuff about Mother Teresa and was very upset that she had stolen my career, even though I intended to give it up. I wanted to be original, and she'd beaten me to it.

My best friend, Lorna, who lived across street, also despised housework, so she promised to head to America with me to become a cowboy. But she didn't sound too convincing. She might have liked the part about going to Hollywood, California, but she wasn't so sure about the cowboy business. I, on the other hand, was quite sure this was what I wanted to do with my life.

I was still caught up in the flurry and fluster at school, thinking about choosing a career. There was a long list to choose from, and the kids at York Town Primary were excitedly looking at the list to see where they fit—lawyer, doctor, nurse, teacher. The list was long, but there was no listing for mother of an orphanage or a cowboy. I didn't seem to fit anywhere on the list. I began to worry and fret, but Sweet Breeze kept intercepting my thoughts with shouts of "Author! Author!" At first I ignored him, because I didn't think he was calling out to me. When he said it again, I looked up into the sky with the saddest how-could-you-be-so-mean-to-me expression on my face. *He thinks I'm a boy.* I felt for the ribbon in my hair. I looked at my uniform then at my shoes. It was my shoes—those stupid boy shoes my mother had bought me. I hated shoes with laces. They looked like boy shoes. I liked shoes with bows or buckles, but my mother said laced-up shoes lasted longer because they held my feet more securely. Now Sweet Breeze was mistaking me for a boy because of them.

I'm a girl! My name is not Arthur! I yelled in my mind at Sweet Breeze. *How could you mistake me for a boy? I am not Arthur. I am not Arthur. You are so way off. There's not even one boy in the entire school by that name. The only Arthur I know is Dake's oldest son, and he's way too old for primary school. So there!* (A boy named Arthur did attend York Town Primary, but he enrolled after this particular episode with Sweet Breeze.)

In retrospect, I realize I got the name Arthur mixed up with the word "author" because they're pronounced similarly in Jamaican patois. The humour in this was lost to me for over a decade until I was writing the first draft of this book some sixteen years later.

CHAPTER SEVEN

Mom's the Word

More time passed, and despite my many attempts to get her to do so, Mrs. Williams refused to give up on me choosing a career in writing. She called me to her classroom to speak to me again about telling my parents to come see her to talk about my future. She asked again if I'd decided on a career, and she reminded me of the importance of making my mark on the world, and so on. I told her I was still undecided. When she was through talking to me, I stormed off to the playground to have another talk with God about my career and future.

I didn't want to be a writer because it would cause people to know me. I was looking forward to a quiet, peaceful life in obscurity. I didn't want to become a writer. I didn't want to be well-known. If I became a writer of any sort, people would know me and point me out in a crowd. They would point at my house when they went by and say, "The person who writes such and such lives there." I wouldn't have any privacy. On the way to the playground, I picked up a stick and made a mark on the ground. "There," I said, "I've made my mark upon the world. Now I can live my life in peace."

I sat under a tree. *God*, I called out without saying a word, *I don't like this world, and I don't want to be anybody in it, but my teachers won't leave me alone.* I reminded God of my original plan to become the mother of an orphanage and my new plans to become a cowboy in Hollywood, California. At this point I wasn't fully aware that there were cameras filming the cowboy movies that inspired me. I thought they were just riding across wide-open country and living free—from housework. Then I felt the familiar stir in the air of Sweet Breeze coming down, and I started to giggle as he tickled me with that sweet, cool, refreshing wind that accompanied him. "How do you always know where to find me, Sweet Breeze?" I giggled as I left Sweet Breeze to continue my talk with God.

I told God I couldn't find a career that was more appropriate for me than being a cowboy, and I reminded him of the deal I'd made with him to get me to Hollywood, California. That's what I saw written on the movie screens, and that's where all the action and adventure began.

"So what's going to happen to the children when you leave?" Sweet Breeze asked.

"Oh, jeez." I was really torn between staying and becoming the mother of an orphanage and running away to become a cowboy. "It pains me to leave them," I agonized. "But I can't stay here. I can't stay here. They're killing me with housework. They're making a domestic fowl out of me. It will be the death of me if I stay." I thought long and hard, then added, "I'll send them pretty things from America." I compromised.

Sweet Breeze responded, "You know, things don't always go as planned."

"I'm going away to America to become a cowboy, and that's that. Who's big enough to stop me?"

Sweet Breeze went into the pregnant pause mode, similar to when I asked him if God was a spirit, so I whistled for my horse, Born Free, and rode away as fast as I could.

Another day, another encounter with Mrs. Williams, and I ran out onto the playground to have another talk with God about my career. "God, we need to talk. You never talk back to me, but we need to talk, because Mrs. Williams won't leave me alone, and all these teachers are telling me that I'm born to be a writer and want to make plans for me to become one, when I know I'm born to be a cowboy."

Sweet Breeze said, "Don't make any plans for your future. You're not going to have a normal life."

"Sweet Breeze! That doesn't make any sense. God, do you hear me? We need to talk, but you never answer me."

"So who's talking to you now?"

"I'm talking to myself. I'm really talking to God, but he never replies. I've almost given up thinking that he ever will, but I still talk to him, because it makes me feel good. He doesn't seem to care about his children on Earth anymore. He's gone up. He's gone up. I know why he's gone up, and I don't blame him. These darn, blasted people down here make too much noise, always cussing and fighting, yelling and screaming at each other, and not doing good. God can't live among that kind of mess. That's why he's gone up. I don't blame him, but he shouldn't have gone up without hearing from me. He should've stuck around until I came then given me a chance to prove myself."

"So who's talking to you now?"

"Sweet Breeze is talking to me."

"Who is Sweet Breeze?"

"Sweet Breeze is me."

Sweet Breeze didn't respond. I knew whenever he didn't respond, it meant he didn't agree with me but wouldn't say so. He remained silent. Pregnant pause, again.

"You don't believe Sweet Breeze is me? Sweet Breeze is me. Sweet Breeze is my conscience. You know when I steal something or tell a lie, how that little voice keeps nagging at me that I did wrong, that little voice always telling me I shouldn't do certain things? Well, that's Sweet Breeze. Sweet Breeze is my higher self. I am talking to my higher self. Now do you believe Sweet Breeze is me?"

"If you say so."

I continued laying out my complaint to God about my plans for my future and the teachers' plans for my career.

After a short pause, Sweet Breeze continued. "You are going to be the mother of God's children when you grow up."

I was puzzled by the word "mother," and, like Bible Mary, I raised my eyebrows and pondered. *Am I going to be like Bible Mary in the future, bearing not only a son but children for God? And how am I going to be able to bear children for God when I grow up if God doesn't even know that I exist? God's gone farther and farther up into the heavens and, according to*

Pastor, may even have become a spirit. Just then, some spirit-filled dancing women with the gift of foresight, women whom everyone in the community called "Mothers," danced across my sight and into full view. I started laughing. *Me? One of those spirit women? You're funny. You're very funny.* I laughed and laughed at Sweet Breeze's joke and sense of humour.

The members of my church looked down their noses on these women. My parents didn't go to church, but they didn't approve of them either, and I certainly didn't like them or anyone who talked about spirit. They were spiritual Mothers who took care of their flock and everyone, for that matter. I was a carefree cowboy. We had absolutely nothing in common.

About the only one who ever used the title "mother" in reference to me was Ya Ya. She called me Mother Miserable. She named me that because sometimes she was at a loss trying to figure out how best to help me. For instance, I went running to her at her house at Top Yard whenever I got into trouble with my mother or father at our house at Bottom Yard. She'd see me running toward her as if someone was after me and ask, "Bev, who's after you now, your mother or your father?"

"My mother."

"Your mother again? What did you do this time?"

"Nothing. I didn't do anything."

"I know you didn't do anything. I don't know why she's always after you to beat you when you didn't do anything. Never mind, mi dear."

"When I grow up, I'm going to have lots and lots of money, and I'm going to buy lots of candy and soda, and I'm not going to give her any."

"That's right, mi dear. Don't give her any. She doesn't deserve any of your candy and soda. She has no right to want to beat you when you didn't do anything wrong."

"Don't say that about my mother. You're going too far."

"But, Bev, I'm on your side, and now you're turning on *me?*"

"Because you're going too far. You're going too far."

"She's my daughter, you know."

"She may be your daughter, but she's my mother, and you're going too far."

Jeez, I thought, *God wouldn't go this far. He'd know exactly where to draw the line. He'd know exactly what to say to make me feel better.*

Or sometimes Ya Ya and Auntie Callie would lay in wait for me as Yvonne and I came home from Sister Betty's school. "Bev, what did you learn in school today?"

I'd be hot, tired, and hungry from the long walk home in the afternoon sun. "Nothing. I learned nothing in school today," I'd yell, stomping my feet. "Every day you ask the same question. I learn nothing."

"We know you learn nothing," they'd say, smiling and winking at each other. "You just go to school to warm the bench and to spend your recess money on candy."

"I don't go to school to warm the bench or to spend the recess money. I don't warm the bench. I learn." I'd proceed to give them a long list of all the things I'd learned in school that day.

When I'd exhausted the list, and my lungs, they'd smile at each other and say, "We knew we'd get you to tell us what you learned in school today." Outsmarted, I'd storm off to my house. And that's why she called me Mother Miserable. I was really a good-natured child, but I could also be very temperamental. Housework made me miserable. Spirit made me miserable. Turning the other cheek made me miserable. And people going too far made me miserable.

Back to Mother. The three things that came to mind whenever I thought of Mother—the women who danced into my view—were first, her dance; second, her attire; and third, her gift of prophecy. Mother loved to dance. In her dance, she made not only her soul boast in the Lord but also her whole being. In short, Mother was a real spiritual reveller. When the congregation sang "When Israel out of Bondage Came,"[11] Mother demonstrated the song in dance the whole way through. She showed how Israel came out of bondage. She demonstrated how God reached down His mighty hand and rolled the sea away, then she showed how the church today should go "forward still" because "it's Jehovah's will though the billows toss and sway" it. Mother swayed with the billows, caught her balance, straightened up to step firmly with a "conquering tread" to "push ahead, for God will roll the sea away." Mother reeled and turned, spun and dipped to the words of the songs.

You just had to make way for Mother, even before she arrived, where you were standing or sitting in her street meetings, and I imagined inside her church as well. When Mother danced, she didn't worry about where she ended up or if she would fall. She just went where the spirit led. Watching Mother dance made me think of the words from the nursery rhyme "I Have a Little Nut Tree," which says, "I dance over water. I dance over sea. And all the birds in the air could not catch me." Mother danced over land and sea.

Mother dressed like an army general, a high priest, and a matron in a hospital all rolled into one. She seemed to favour the colours red, white, gold, purple, or blue. With her long, navy blue, red, or white dress, Mother wore sensible shoes and socks, complemented by a gold or red sash around her waist, an intricately wrapped headdress, with her rod in hand.

Mother held the hem of her skirt and danced with wild abandon both at home and abroad. She put her hands on her hips and did a local dance, turned, reeled, and came forward. She spun and danced backward with her eyes closed, but she never fell. The crowd parted like the Red Sea to let her through as she danced in the spirit. She danced across the waters and over the seas, grabbed a partner and did an Irish or Scottish jig or, with hands akimbo, an African spin. Mother was a multicultural, international spirit dancer. Like Bible David, Mother loved to dance in the presence of the Lord.

One of those Mothers lived at Four Paths, which was about a mile away from Content. I knew her only as Mother at Four Paths or Four Paths Mother. She held church services in her yard next to her house. I used to pass her house on my way to and from Four Paths Primary. She had a shop at her gate, from which she sold grated coconut cakes, coconut drops, and other sweets. I avoided buying anything from her shop and crossed to the other side of the street to avoid walking where she walked. I'd never met Mother at Four Paths, and I didn't even know her name. But one thing I knew for sure was that I didn't like her because I assumed she was a spirit woman who talked about spirit.

My mother had told me about the time her best friend asked her to go with her to visit Mother at Four Paths. While they were on their way to Mother's house, my mother said to her friend, "I'm only going with you because you're my friend, but I don't believe a word these people say."

When they arrived at Mother's gate, they saw her standing there, waiting for them. Mother at Four Paths said to my mother, "Don't come into my yard. You said you don't believe anything I say." My mother had to stay outside the gate and wait for her friend. To this day, my mother is still trying to figure out how Mother at Four Paths knew what she had said about her on the way.

Then there was Mother Ritty, who lived closer to home. I passed her house almost every day whenever we took the shortcut across the canals and by the railway tracks on our way to and from York Town Primary. I first met her when I was still in Sister Betty's school. My baby cousin, Tony, had been sick and showed no sign of improvement, despite many trips to the doctor. I was on the delicate side myself, so when a car showed up one day to take Tony to the doctor, and my mother said I was going to the doctor also, I was more than excited to go for a ride in the car. Somehow, they had a change of mind, and the car ended up at Mother Ritty's house. I came out cussing under my breath that I was tricked into going into the spirit woman's yard. My mother knew she couldn't get me there any other way. My mother and my aunt didn't have much faith in these women, but I guess Tony's illness was getting worse, and they were really desperate for help.

I was always sick—not any major illness, just puny and weak from throwing up, sometimes to the point of lying in bed and looking like I was about to die. I had a severe allergy to milk and eggs, which I avoided. But the smallest trace of it on someone, or on a plate or cup that wasn't washed thoroughly, could send me into convulsive fits of emptying the contents of my stomach. I guess it didn't help my situation any that I'd seen, cussed out, and fought a few invisible people. So my mother figured she had nothing to lose by taking me along.

I looked around the spirit woman's yard, hoping to find something to justify my feelings toward her and her kind. She had flowers planted all over. The flowers were surrounded by stones painted white, spelling out the words Love, Peace, Hope, and so forth. Then Mother Ritty came out to greet us, and I started cussing her under my breath: "You better not touch me with your unclean hands. Don't look at me. Don't come near me. You're unclean. You're unclean." But as the petite woman got closer, she smiled, and her smile and serene demeanour disarmed me. There was an air of peace and tranquility about her.

She looked at Tony first, because he was very sick. She said he wasn't going to make it and told my aunt the reason. She said they should have come to her sooner. Tony died soon after.

Then she looked at me. I can't fully describe the way Mother Ritty reacted as she looked me over. She got all excited, as though she were seeing and saluting an old friend, but I didn't get the feeling that I was the old friend. Then Mother Ritty exclaimed, "It's not an evil spirit! It's not an evil spirit! It's not an evil spirit! It's not an evil spirit that's troubling her. She is okay. She's going to be just fine."

I left Mother Ritty with a smile on my face, thinking, *That's right. It's not an evil spirit. It's not an evil spirit. No evil spirit can come near me, because I am the Spirit Fighter. I am a real good spirit fighter.*

Thereafter, I had a modicum of respect for Mother Ritty, but not enough to go near her house. When I was around ten years old, my classmate Lurline, one of Mother Ritty's adopted daughters, asked me to accompany her home at lunchtime because she had forgotten her lunch money. I told her I'd go with her but would wait for her by the canal. I said this because I didn't want to go into her yard and risk having to say good afternoon to Mother Ritty or have her look at or talk to me. I sat on the concrete partition of the floodgate in the middle of the canal beside their house and swished my feet back and forth in the water until Lurline returned.

When I was around ten years old, one of these spiritual Mothers showed up at our gate one Saturday morning. She came in the yard and told Ya Ya that the Lord had sent her. She asked Ya Ya, "Do you have a little girl here who is always throwing up?" Before Ya Ya could answer, all the kids in the yard shouted, "That's Bev!"

Mother, whom we recognized only by her calm demeanour and commanding sense of purpose, asked Ya Ya for a not-too-desirable ingredient and proceeded to boil some tea for me. *Yuck,* I thought. She looked at me and said, "Don't bother making that funny face. Drink."

I held my breath and drank, and the issue of constantly throwing up disappeared, never to return. That mother wasn't from the community. No one knew her, and she knew no one, yet she knew that I had a problem most people in the community didn't know. She knew where to find me and that I'd be cured, even though she never returned to find out.

There were other spiritual Mothers whom I didn't really know because they just came and went at various times to hold open-air meetings at night. They'd just show up in the evenings, just before sunset or thereabouts, announcing they had a message or a warning from God for Content. These words were sometimes for an individual or a family or the community. The distinct warning sound of drums beating loudly coming down the lane, usually just before or after sunset, announced the arrival of Mother and her entourage. And there was no mistaking who was Mother. She was the one decorated with badges like a war general, dressed like a priest from the Old Testament, rod in hand, spinning, dancing, groaning, shouting, and laughing. Mother usually introduced herself and her respective church during the meetings, but I don't remember where they were from.

These were the spirit women, the Mothers, I had in mind when I started laughing at Sweet Breeze's joke. They didn't wear high heels because they danced, spun, and twirled. They spoke in tongues and prophesied about future events or about secret things people were planning or doing against each other. They were strong, powerful women, the type who could put their feet down and order God to bed to rest on Sundays after church. Even the men in their entourage, and in my community, acquiesced to Mother. Mother was not shy. In fact, I classified them as real spiritual revellers. They weren't afraid to walk, talk, and dance in the spirit, with or without an audience. They exulted in the spirit. They were nothing like me. In fact, they were the opposite of me. That's why I found Sweet Breeze's joke so funny.

I laughed so long and hard at the word "Mother" that I missed the most important word in Sweet Breeze's sentence. In the middle of my laughter, I remembered and stopped abruptly. "Wait a minute. Did you say *God?*" I gulped in fear. Sweet Breeze did not reply, and I didn't wait for one. "Aaaah!" I ran off screaming. Fear and dread came over me. Sweet Breeze had never mentioned God before.

When I reached close to the water tank, halfway between the school and the playground, Sweet Breeze called out after me. "Don't start running. You can't escape." I looked back to where the voice was coming from but saw no one, just empty space. Fear ran up my spine, and I shuddered. Still running, I covered my ears with both hands to block out what I was hearing. Sweet Breeze was speaking in a new way—a loud voice with no one visible.

I swiftly rubbed my ears with both hands, wiping out what I heard in my mind. *Bev, this never happened. You didn't hear anything.* I went back to my class and never went back to the playground to talk to God again for the rest of my time at York Town Primary.

One evening just before I entered Denbigh Junior Secondary School, one of those dancing Mother women came to Content with her church to hold an open-air meeting. As usual, a large crowd turned out in anticipation of the Mother's lively church singing, dancing, and prophecies. I went with my sibling and cousins along with the crowd to watch the women and the men in Mother's church for pretty much the same reason I liked to watch Dinah in my church: entertainment. Mother didn't disappoint. Along with her congregants, she sang and danced till heaven came down. Her church was far livelier than the one we attended. In fact, whenever we played church at home, it was her church that we imitated, with Yvonne, of course, playing the role of Mother.

I also wanted to hear Mother's word from God for the members of the community to see if it would come to pass in the coming months, because it always did. After the praise and worship and much dancing, Mother, looking up to the sky, began to prophesy. Her message was for a young girl and contained some hard stuff I didn't want to hear. I barely paid attention to the part where she said, "Touch her not, for she is mine, thus saith the Lord. I will hear her cries and I will fight her battles for her."

Something inside of me kept saying, *This message is for you.* But my mind argued, *It's not for me.* I was thrilled at the thought that God said I was his, even though I didn't see much evidence in my life that God knew I existed. Surely I wouldn't be so poor if God knew me.

Then Mother said, "This child says her prayers every night."

Inwardly, I argued, *That could be anybody. Me, my sister, brother, and cousins have to say our prayers every night before we go to bed. That could apply to them as well.*

As if she could hear me, Mother replied, "This child loves to sing." With that, I snuck away and moved in a semicircle through the large crowd gathered in the square and slipped to the back of the crowd. I made my way through the thick crowd and across the street over to Brother Ken's shop, where the crowd was also thick, observing Mother's meeting in the jam-packed intersection known as Content Square. There were people everywhere, so I kept saying, "Excuse me, excuse me," until there was far enough distance between Mother and me to ease my discomfort. Mother wasn't looking at me, and there was no indication that she was aware of my presence, but her words were getting too close for my comfort.

Singing church hymns and choruses was the only way I could get through cleaning the house or doing the laundry on the weekend without shedding a bucket of tears. I would open the hymnbook on the dining table and go back to it every now and then to get a new song to sing, and pretty soon I was transported from the drudgery of housework into another realm. My heart would find peace as I sang, and a sweet feeling would take over. I also sang a lot of other types of songs every day as well. I didn't have a great voice, but that couldn't hold me back from singing all over the yard.

As soon as I reached the back of the crowd in front of Brother Ken's shop, Mother started spinning like a top in a straight line with her eyes closed. The crowd opened up to let her through. She stopped spinning right in front of me, grabbed my hand, and brought me back to where she was standing in front of her church group, almost to the spot I had been before I snuck off. She then proceeded to anoint, wash, or cover me all over from my head to my feet, back and front, with the Bible. I didn't know what she was doing, only that she placed the Bible all over me.

Then Mother ordered me to dance with her—the very dance that caused me to laugh so uncontrollably at Sweet Breeze's juxtaposition of my career and hers. I hesitated, but Mother was waiting and wouldn't take no for an answer. Someone beside me said, "Dance, Bev." And I danced. Mother wouldn't leave until I joined her in her dance, so I danced until she was somewhat satisfied. I couldn't do the moves like her, so she won the dance-off by a good mile.

I put most of that night out of my mind. I wanted to believe, as she'd said, that God had said I was his, because it meant that God knew me. But since there was no real evidence of this before or after the words she had spoken, I had to put that idea out of my mind too. I still wasn't in America, and nothing good seemed to be happening for me. But I cannot, to this day, fathom how that woman, spinning with her eyes closed, was able to find me in a large crowd in a dark village square. That was impossible to do on a human level.

Mother spoke other words that I don't want to divulge at this time because they contain the other half, the bad half, of my story, which inevitably happens to all of God's people. But suffice to say, I watched Mother's prophecy come true over the course of my life—the bitter with the sweet.

By the time I entered Denbigh Junior Secondary, I no longer remembered the little girl who wanted to be a Bible person. And I most definitely no longer wanted to become a cowboy in Hollywood, California. I hitched a ride on a mule when I was about ten years old and it turned out to be the most painful ride of my life. I realized right then and there on top of that mule that the cowboy life wasn't all it was cracked up to be. I really wanted to ride a horse, but they were in short supply in my community.

Riding on the back of a mule beat walking to Heart Ease, where my mother had sent me on an errand to her Uncle Willie's house. There were no bicycles available, and I protested walking there. A woman on a mule came down from the hills in Clarendon on Fridays to sell her yams and potatoes to us on the plains, so my mother asked if she was going to Heart

Ease. When she replied in the affirmative, my mother asked if she could give me a ride there. Against my better judgement of riding on a lowly domestic mule instead of a fast, clever horse, I jumped on.

Perched on top of the mule behind the higgler, I not only had to endure the laughter and jeers of my companions along the way, but also the pain. Oh, the awful pain each time the mule moved its hind legs. After what seemed like forever, I got off the mule at Uncle Willie's, and for a good while I couldn't walk or talk. I sat in shock and pain. There, on top of that mule, my dreams of becoming a cowboy died. It was a mule, but surely a ride on a mule couldn't be that much different from a ride on a horse.

I was also starting to realize that the cowboy life as portrayed in the movies and on television was all an act in front of cameras. I loved action, but I didn't like lights or cameras. The movies and television shows were also switching from cowboy movies to more family-based dramas and sitcoms. It seemed the cowboy era was long past. We just got the movies and television shows late in Jamaica.

But my heart was still set on running away to America. The movies, TV shows, and magazines were now the window through which I viewed the new America. I "borrowed"—took home, read under my bed, and returned without her knowledge—Miss Mavis's American magazines, such as *True Confessions* and *True Romance*. I "borrowed" them because they were young adult or adult magazines that weren't meant for my age. I loved to read them because they provided me an escape to America. I read so many that I was thoroughly immersed in family life in the USA. The homes had washing machines. I saw a washing machine at Mr. Brown's house. He was related to Mr. Terrier by marriage. They were White, or near White, and rich. They could buy anything.

The teens in the magazines were sophomores and seniors in high school. The girls joined pep squads, and their boyfriends were jocks on the school's sports teams. I didn't want to be a cheerleader, but I was hung up on the word "sophomore." I definitely wanted to be a sophomore in high school. I wanted to go to New York to dress in the latest fashion and go dancing at the nightclubs, and I wouldn't mind going to Hollywood to have a peek at the movie stars.

However, along with these desires, I couldn't shake the feeling of guilt for not wanting to work with unwanted or underprivileged children anymore. Our class was given a list of topics to choose from to write a composition. It was a repetition of an old exercise from primary school.

I didn't like any of the topics, so I decided to tackle the one I'd been putting off over the years: What would you like to be when you grow up? I wrote about how I had avoided the topic because I was never really sure what I wanted to be, and although still uncertain, I knew I'd be working with underprivileged children. I wrote about how I hated to use the word "underprivileged" to describe these children, because they were diamonds in the rough. Just like real diamonds, they were waiting for someone to dig through the dirt to find them, clean them up, and make them shine.

Miss Samuels, my homeroom teacher who was also my social studies teacher, then began to bother me about my career and school attendance. She suspected I was having financial problems. She told our class she wasn't rich but was willing to help a student financially, and that she was available to meet with anyone after school if they needed to talk to her. I knew that her invitation was meant for me. I usually arrived at school late each morning because I never got much sleep at night and always got up feeling tired. And by the time I finished crying my way through household chores, all the morning buses were gone. There was no sense waiting for the later buses, as they ran about every hour or so after rush hour. Denbigh was less than two miles away, so it made sense to walk whenever I missed the early buses. My only hope was to catch up with my classmates, Ione and Iona. Ione lived up the lane and Iona on Foga Road. Like me, they were generally late. If we were really lucky, Ione's dad or brother would give us a ride to school. Most mornings, though, we just tried to slip into the schoolyard by taking a shortcut across the railway, making sure the principal didn't see us.

Miss Samuels took attendance each morning and marked me present, even when I wasn't there. She knew I was always late. She sensed something was wrong and wanted to help in any way she could. She feared it was only a matter of time before I quit school, so she encouraged me to stay in school. On days when our last class of the day ended in our homeroom, I sensed Miss Samuels hurrying to get to our class before we left so she could have a talk with me. But before class would end, I'd pack up my books and run out. I'd see her coming and would hide so she wouldn't see me. I had two problems bothering me, but I didn't see the point of talking to her about them, as I believed my life would be ending soon.

The first was that my lunch money wasn't enough. My mother or father gave me what they thought was enough lunch money for the week, but there was a small problem. They expected me to leave early to get to school on time by walking there, but there was a stigma attached to students who walked to school unless they lived close by. They were looked down on and referred to as the "walk-foot" kids or kids who took the "foot-mobile." I wasn't going to be one of the "walk-foot" kids. When I was on time, I paid my fare and got on the bus with the other kids. This left me with even less money for lunch and recess. As a result, I usually missed a day or two of school—Thursdays and Fridays—because I used the lunch money on bus fare and had no money left to get to school or to buy lunch, so I stayed home.

The next problem was that I was having dark and terrible recurring dreams at night. I dreamed about holes suddenly opening up in the ground in front of me, and I saw myself falling into them. Then it would change to seeing myself being chased by bloodhounds on my way home from school. These dreams were surrounded by so much darkness that I just knew they couldn't hold anything good for me. Each night I fell into the dark hole, and I'd grab hold of the root of a tree in the hole to prevent myself from falling to the bottom. I'd hang on, crying out for help. Someone above would come and throw me a rope, glowing as if it were made of light, and pull me up. When I'd get out of the hole, I'd look for the person to say thanks, but no one would be there.

Night after night, dogs with long fangs would chase me on my way home from school, ready to rip me to pieces, and I'd run down my street to get home. As they'd be about to close in on me, a tree would spring up out of the earth and I'd climb up and be saved. Most of the time, though, the dogs would chase me and I'd run to Mother at Four Paths, screaming for her to help me. There was a gully beside Mother's house, and I'd run across it to get to her, while the dogs would stay on the other side, afraid to come any closer.

The dreams ended with me on Mother's side of the gully, out of breath and crying, looking at the mad dogs glaring at me. Mother herself was never in the dreams. I was having a hard time understanding why I was running to her for help when I'd never even met her, and I most certainly did not like her.

As if the nights weren't scary enough, I was also seeing things before they happened. I'd be sitting or standing and a vision—like a movie—would start unfolding before my eyes, only to happen in the future. These dreams and occurrences pointed to one thing: I was going to die soon, and God was warning me through dreams and visions that my time was ending.

I was looking out the classroom window one day and wondering what was happening to me and how long it would be before I died. Miss Samuels saw me and warned, "Stop daydreaming about quitting school and going out into the world, Beverley. You won't fit in. You're not meant for that. Don't take your gift of writing too lightly. God gave you that gift for a reason." She tried her best to encourage me to stay.

She tried to get me involved in class debates and other stuff, but I was so far gone in my belief that I was about to die that her words couldn't save me. I didn't join in the discussion, but to help my team out, I wrote a reply and slipped it under the desk to a teammate. She used it to argue her point. Miss Samuels responded, "That's from Beverley. Beverley your writing has a voice, you know."

What? I thought to myself. *My writing has a voice? I thought only speech had a voice.*

Miss Samuels did all she could to make me feel as though I belonged in school, but nothing seemed to work. As a last resort, she tried a game. She led the class in clapping and singing: "Those who were born in January, skip around." At that point, students who were born in January got up and skipped around the class. She went through all the months of the year, but I didn't move from my desk. Still determined to see me be a part of the class, she sang, "Those who were never born skip around. Those who were never born skip around. Tra-la-la-la-la-la-la. Those who were never born skip around." That elicited a smile from me that turned to laughter, and the class joined in the laughter. We shared a good moment of fun, but I was still not convinced to come back to life and be a part of the class.

"Bev, I know you're shy, but don't go to Denbigh and hide your talent. Don't fade into the background. Keep shining through your writing. Keep up the good work, okay?" Those were Mrs. Williams's parting words to me on leaving York Town Primary for Denbigh Junior Secondary. But it wasn't about being shy or fading away. It was about horrible nightmares and the sense of foreboding they engendered.

It was our free period to catch up on schoolwork. The class prefect or second prefect was in charge. The prefects were responsible for recording and reporting our behaviour to the teachers at any time, but especially during free period. I looked up from my desk to see everyone eagerly engaging in group research in the Bible. *What miracle hath Captain wrought in my absence among these thirteen- and fourteen-year-olds to make them so interested in the Bible?* I wondered. Captain was our religious knowledge teacher, but he came to our class on the days I missed school, so I hardly saw him. I was used to Bentley belting out "If I Had a Hammer" and the class joining in, or Laxton and the other popular boys singing "Oh Cecilia" to make the girls blush, but now they were frantically turning and searching the pages of the Bible. I wanted to join in the fun and banter then, but the only song that seemed to reverberate with me was "The Sound of Silence."

"What's going on?" I asked, deeply puzzled to see them all so very captivated by the Bible.

"We're looking for love verses."

"What? In the Bible? There are love verses in the Bible?" That's the last place I expected to see them, but that explained everything.

"Yup! Tons of them."

"Where?"

"In the Song of Solomon."

"Let me see. I have to see this to believe it." Between Sunday school, school, church, and home, I had pretty much read through most of the

Bible. I was pretty sure I had read the Song of Solomon before, but I didn't recall seeing any love verses. I joined in their search for love verses. The imagery was somewhat confusing, but I found some good lines by picking here and there. I added a few of my own to their collection that I'd copied from a friend: "I've fallen from the highest mountain. I've fallen into the deepest sea, but the greatest fall I ever had was when I fell in love with you."

"Wow! That's a good one. Where'd you get it?"

"From a friend. She has a whole book full of them."

"Do you have any more?"

"Yup."

While my classmates were busy discussing plans for their future and searching for love verses to write to their beloved, I was busy writing away at my desk near the window at the back of the class. Morning, noon, and afternoon, every spare moment after completing each subject, I went back to writing. *Crick!* I looked up to see the entire class smiling at me. "What?"

"You do this every day. You're not even aware of it. You write like crazy then stretch your hand. Your elbow makes a popping sound and you go right back to writing and stretching your hand every now and then, without looking up."

That day I was busy writing what sounded like half love letter, half letter to someone in the universe for help. "Dear _____, Do you really care about me? Do you even know that I exist?" My letter got confiscated by the teacher, who thought it was the beginning of a love letter.

"Imagine that," she said to the class, "she's busy writing a love letter while I'm trying to teach."

Giggles, giggles, giggles.

Meanwhile, over in the science lab as we studied the human body, I was equally amazed and repulsed at the various organs, blood vessels, and so forth that made up the human body. I looked at the heart and the arteries that carried the blood all over the body, and they made me realize how beautiful and vulnerable the human body is. It was a fine piece of machinery dependent on food, water, and air to keep it alive. I realized how unfortunate it would be if God were made of flesh, because flesh was so susceptible to injury that even the prick of a pin could put God out of commission. In the science lab of Denbigh Junior Secondary, I was ready to accept the fact that God was indeed a spirit.

Over the past couple of years, I'd been slowly coming around to the possibility that God may indeed be a spirit. That day, I willingly accepted that he was. I still needed time to come to terms with this new way of seeing God, but flesh was simply too weak and vulnerable to be the stuff God was made of. However, I was also convinced that he was going to take away my life. God was not going to take my life away because he was a spirit, but because my number was up.

I was late for school again. I was not in a good mood when I was late, as I wanted to be on time. But most mornings I got up with little or no sleep because of the recurring dark dreams. So, still tired and sleepy, and while getting the water together for breakfast and my bath, I'd see Dolsie, her sisters, and her cousins going by on their way to school. They walked to school, so they were up at the crack of dawn to do their chores and get to school on time. My mother reminded me over and over that if they could do it, so could I. But my body was tired, and my mind said I didn't belong with the foot soldiers or walk-foot students. I belonged with the upper-class students who took the bus to school. I was late for the bus, so getting to school on time via the foot-mobile was unlikely.

On top of waking up tired, I had to make breakfast for the family. I cussed and cried as I prepared the meal before setting off for school. And then I cussed and cried some more when I missed the bus.

One morning I was having no luck at all. I missed the bus, and both Ione and Iona were already gone. I walked to school by myself. I didn't take the shortcut, because I didn't think it was safe to do so alone. Walking the mile and a half to school alone gave me more time to cuss and cry about how unfair my life was. I had little lunch money, because we'd always been poor, but we were even poorer than we used to be because my parents had split up and there was a new baby.

After such a long walk, I only felt relief as I got closer to school. But this relief turned to worry about whether I'd be fortunate enough to escape a visit with the principal for coming to school late. That would be compounded by his scrutiny of everything I was wearing, from the hair on my head to the socks and shoes on my feet, but especially my uniform. Everything had to be neat and clean and in its proper place. I wasn't very good at ironing my uniform, and after a mile and a half of dust and sweat, I was afraid this tardy foot soldier wouldn't pass the test.

If morning assembly, or morning devotion as it was called, was over and the students had dispersed to their respective classes, the school gate would be closed. Then I'd have to make sure the coast was clear before throwing my schoolbag over the high fence, hooking my shoes on the fence's mesh wire, and climbing up and jumping over—a handy skill left over from the days when I was preparing for my career as a cowboy. I would then have to run and hide around the back of the first of the three buildings that comprised Denbigh Junior Secondary until I reached the girls' washroom. Once there, I'd check my schedule to see where my class was and decide whether it was safe to stay there till next class, when I could slip out and join up with my classmates as they proceeded to the next class, or go to my class undetected by the principal.

Even if I made it safely to class for first period, I still wasn't home free. Depending on the teacher that morning, I could be sent to the principal's office to explain why I was late or be subject to the chant of the boys sitting in the front row of my class: "Late for school, late for church, late for your wedding, you'll even be late for your own funeral."

One time I stepped angrily in response to their chants and stomped into the classroom, threw my books on my desk, and flopped down noisily on my chair. The teacher ordered me out of the classroom, saying, "Beverley, please go out that door and return to your seat and sit down like a proper young lady." While the boys giggled, I was forced to retrace my steps, put my books away quietly, fold the pleats of my skirt, and sit down nicely on my chair.

That was the mood I was in that morning, cussing and crying because I was late yet again, and not sure what to expect when I arrived at school. As I drew near Denbigh Commons, the area between Denbigh Primary and Denbigh Junior Secondary, something within me forced me to look at the sky. For a brief second, I saw the upper part of a man's body jutting out of a bright cloud, with his hand extended toward me, saying, "Here, take my hand. I want to help you."

I yelled, "I am not taking your hand! I am not taking your hand! My life is a mess. I have to make breakfast for everyone before I can leave for school. I missed the bus. I'm late for school again. If the principal sees me, I'm in big trouble. I don't have enough lunch money. *Surely goodness and mercy shall follow me all the days of my life…* is this surely goodness and mercy? Is this surely goodness and mercy? Why did you have to make me so poor? Is this your idea of goodness and mercy? I'm only thirteen years old. What did I ever do in my short life to deserve this? And now you want to take my life. Go ahead and take my life. I don't care anymore."

Crying, and without so much as a glance upward, I stormed off toward school. The gate was locked, so I checked to ensure no one was looking, threw my bag over the fence, made the climb very few girls would attempt, and headed straight for the girls' washroom to wait for the opportune time to join up with my class.

Yvonne had confided in me that she and her friends found out that they could stretch their lunch money by purchasing lunch from street vendors over at Denbigh Commons. These vendors sold food mainly to the Denbigh Primary students. Purchasing food from vendors wasn't a classy thing to do for the older students. The kids at Denbigh Junior Secondary, and especially those in my class, wouldn't be caught dead buying food from vendors. They didn't even consider it cool to purchase hot lunch from our school cafeteria, let alone buy food from the vendors who sold outside the school gates. Only the poorer kids did that.

Our school was divided into roughly eighteen classes of grade seven, eight, and nine students, according to age and academic abilities. The classy thing to do for lunch was to go to Miss Suzie's shop and buy beef patties and coco bread and wash it down with chocolate milk or soda, then top it all off with an ice cream cone. I couldn't afford any of that. I couldn't even afford to buy a hot lunch at the school cafeteria. My lunch money was way behind what the average student received from their parents, and after splurging on bus fare to avoid being associated with the foot-mobile crowd, I had little left. At recess, I bought a freezie, or "kisko pop" as we called it, to quench my thirst from walking from home to school, or to calm the rumble in my stomach because I didn't like to eat breakfast. There was hardly anything left after all that. So buying at Miss Suzie's was out of the question.

Miss Samuels, our homeroom teacher, imparted to us the importance of a hot lunch. She tried to ensure we paid for and had our names on the list for hot lunches from the school cafeteria before she left our homeroom in the mornings. The students went along with her idea to appease her, only to toss out the hot lunch and head for Miss Suzie's at lunchtime. Miss Samuels was aware that I didn't make the lunch list often, and she knew it was because I couldn't afford it. She encouraged us to come and see her if we didn't have lunch money, but pride wouldn't allow me to "beg" for food, even though I often wished I could have the food tossed in the garbage. So I took to sneaking across to Denbigh Commons at lunchtime to buy food, all the while pretending I was going for a leisurely stroll on the pretty green grass.

As I snuck across Denbigh Commons one afternoon, I was in a rare good mood, because I had finally gotten the white sneakers I had begged, cried, and pleaded with my mother to purchase for me from the Bata shoe store. I was feeling good. Finally. I looked like one of the cool, classy kids. White running shoes and bobby socks were in. They were all the rage at school. They were cool. They were our statement against our extremely strict principal, Mr. Bryan, and something we could do to his face and get away with. He had ordered us to wear black shoes and navy blue socks, but the physical education uniform called for white sneakers and bobby socks that we could wear to school on days when our class had P.E.

The girls all thought the teeny bopper style—white sneakers and bobby socks— was way cooler than black shoes and navy blue socks. And so it was P.E. every day, because Mr. Bryan couldn't tell who was having P.E. on any given day. However, he eventually caught on as the fashion spread throughout the school, and he concluded from the number that so many girls couldn't be having P.E. on the same day. So he ordered us back into black and navy blue.

But before he caught on, I was wearing my hard-won pair of sneakers and stepping like the cool kids as I strolled over to Denbigh Commons. Just as I got to the spot where I'd seen the hand jutting out from the sky, I had a nasty slip and fell to the ground amid laughter. It had rained the night before, the grass was slippery, and there were mud puddles. My white sneakers and socks and my aquamarine blue uniform and white blouse were now a muddy brown. Just as I was about to cry, wondering what I was going to do, Joy, one of Sa'ma's (short for Sister Mama, whose real name was Sister Miller) daughters, walked by. She said, "Bev, I'm going over to Sister Shirley's house to eat my lunch. Why don't you come with me and ask Sister Shirley if you can wash and iron your uniform there?" Joy brought her lunch from home, and because it wasn't cool to do so, ate it in the safety of Sister Shirley's home where the kids at school couldn't see and make fun of her. Help just in the nick of time. I gladly went with Joy.

Sister Shirley gave me lunch and a change of clothes and then showed me where to wash my uniform. I guess she realized I was no good at the washing, starching, and ironing business. My hands were so skinny that people often wondered if I had enough strength in them to wash or iron, and I guess Sister Shirley wondered that too. She took my uniform and washed and added some starch to it, while I took care of washing my socks and sneakers. She hung it out to dry in the sun, but it wasn't anywhere near dry by the time Joy was ready to return to school. So I stayed at Sister Shirley's instead of going back to school after lunch. When my uniform was almost dry, she ironed it for me. I returned to school just before classes were over to get my books and homework. Everyone admired my clean, newly ironed uniform, some wondering how I managed to keep it so clean and wrinkle-free all day. I'd never looked better at school.

I felt good all the way home. Not only did I look good, but I also didn't have to wash and iron my uniform when I got home. I just had to hang it up for school the next day. On the way home from school, close to Jacob Hut, I saw an upper-class boy being driven home from school by his mother. He didn't go to Denbigh Junior Secondary, that was for sure. He probably attended Glen Muir High. I hoped he saw me in my clean, freshly ironed uniform. He was the kind of boy I'd love to send a love letter to. His mother wouldn't approve of me, and neither would he, but I didn't care. Sister Shirley had cleaned me up real good, and I was feeling bold enough to take on both of them.

I found some money on the road, beside the grass where I had fallen. I went home bragging how I was going to eat in style at school the next day because I had found some money. However, I woke up to discover that my mother had cut me down to my usual lunch allowance, stating she was stretching it to make it last longer. I'd spent the whole evening dreaming of eating at Miss Suzie's like the cool kids and was so looking forward to going to school feeling rich and cool. Now I was back to being poor and uncool. I decided that the best revenge was to cry loudly all the way to Lane Head and let everyone know what my mother had done, hoping they would side with me.

I started my wailing, and my first sympathizer, Miss Evelyn, asked, "Bev, what's wrong?" I was about to reply to her when, for no reason, I just started digging through garbage on the street with my shoe on my foot. In the rubble of sugarcane leaves and other debris, I saw the equivalent of what my mother had taken of my lunch money. I stopped crying, picked it up quickly, and ran off to school, without bothering to explain to Miss Evelyn. I could still dine in style. I got to school and could hardly wait for lunchtime.

Lunchtime came around, and I marched off with the cool kids to Miss Suzie's to buy a beef patty, a coco bread, and a chocolate milk. I was hanging with the cool kids, eating at Miss Suzie's, and feeling good, but my stomach was thinking differently. It wasn't used to having a proper lunch. I ran outside and emptied my stomach. Not cool. Not cool at all.

My terrible recurring dreams continued, and they caused me to believe they were signs I was going to die. Yet again I was being chased by three bloodhounds, and I ran over a mile from Content to Mother at Four Paths, yelling for Mother to help me and taking a shortcut across the gully rather than risking going the extra distance to her gate and then up to her house.

In another dream, the bloodhounds were waiting for me at my gate as I returned home from school in the dark after staying for extra lessons in preparation to sit the upcoming exams. The dogs chased me down my street as I yelled to God for help. Again, a tree suddenly sprung up out of the earth, allowing me to climb to safety as the dogs growled and yapped below.

In another recurring dream, I was walking in the dark, and the ground beneath my feet suddenly opened and swallowed me. I screamed out, "God, help me! Help me, God!" as I tumbled into the hole. The now-familiar root appeared again, and I held on for dear life. The figure appeared again, threw me a rope made of light, and told me to take hold of the rope while pulling me up. I did as the person said, but when I emerged from the dark hole, I was alone.

I took these dreams to mean that my life on Earth was shortly coming to an end. I got angry with God and yelled, "You've given me a terrible life so far, and now you're going to cut it short. You're going to take my life. You're going to kill me. Go ahead, I don't care anymore. You've given me a rotten deal so far."

Then one day, in the middle of learning about the birds and the bees, and of budding puppy love romances at school, I quit school and went home to die.

And that's when the burnings began.

FULL CIRCLE

I've written about the burnings and many of the extraordinary things that have happened in my life, but there's a bit more to my story. There are also a few individuals whose presence on my journey has been invaluable and who have contributed to making this book what it is.

God, my Sweet Breeze: Father God, thank you. You are indeed faithful and true. You called me, and I ran out of fear and disobedience for a long time, but you came and made me laugh. The literal search for David's sandal made me one of the few children in primary school who could list archaeology as one of their favourite subjects. It's off my mantelpiece and on my feet, for now there is only one thing I desire of the Lord, and that will I seek after, that I may dwell in the house of the Lord all the days of my life and behold the beauty of the Lord and inquire in his temple (Psalm 27:4).

I am no longer embarrassed by Jesus's Bible story. It now makes sense on so many levels. Something big did happen in Jerusalem that day. There was war in Gethsemane, and there was indeed a very big showdown at the cross. Calvary was the place of the ultimate spiritual fighting. I am now proud of the cross and the victory won at Calvary. I exult in the cross. I glory in the cross. I flourish in the cross and the Christmas message of peace on earth, goodwill to all.

As I sensed, Jesus's Bible story is not complete, but not because he didn't do a good job. He did an excellent job. He folded death's clothes and put on eternity. Jesus didn't go down "like that." He ascended on high. The dark, empty tomb is now flooded with light, because I not only heard about Jesus in Sunday school and church, or read about him in the pages of the Bible, but I also saw him ascend and descend to and from the heavens with my eyes. He did not go out "like that"; instead, he came into my heart. And now I feel him ascending and descending in my heart and my spirit.

You sent Jesus back to continue his Bible story with me and whoever says yes to you. The cross, the resurrection, and the ascension are not the end of his story. Because of Jesus's story, I am now planted in the house of the Lord to flourish—in every sense of the word—in his courts, not just in the bushes at Top Yard. Like the captain, I am no longer in exile. I have found my haven of rest because you took the worst Bible story ever and gave me the best Bible story ever. This has to be the best Bible story ever.

Thank you, Sweet Breeze, for bringing me up. It's been quite a journey, especially in light of the knowledge that yours was the voice my mother heard before I could speak and invite God to Jamaica. I entered this world as a sick baby who couldn't digest formula. My mother tried various brands of formula with the same results—vomiting and diarrhea and my skin breaking out in sores all over. The doctors couldn't diagnose the problem. The last doctor gave up on me and told my mother to take me home and prepare herself for the worst. In his words, "There's nothing physically wrong with her. She's simply refusing to eat. It's as if she doesn't want to stay with us. I don't think she's going to be with us much longer."

But as my mother got off the bus in deep sorrow at Lane Head, she heard a voice say, "The child is, like you, allergic to cow's milk. She is not going to die. Go home and make her porridge with coconut milk."

God, you heard me before I called. You met me at Lane Head long before I called. You knew the direction to Lane Head long before I could give it. Now, through the Hubble telescope via the internet, I watch the marble games you play in space with the planets, moons, stars, and galaxies. From this perspective, it's even more amazing that you heard and found me. Oh my God, you are indeed the Great I Am. And, thank you for the "burnings." As you later revealed to me: the enemy and jealous, evil people around me, were trying to destroy my life. The "burnings" among other things, was necessary to keep me praying and crying out for your help. Thank you for protecting me while I was running away from you.

Yvonne: Yvonne and I were inseparable well into our teen years, and people automatically assumed we were sisters. Yvonne was the loud, noisy half who often spoke for me. Whenever anyone saw one of us, they would ask about the other.

Yvonne and I were like night and day. She was loud, strong, muscular, and outgoing, and I was puny, quiet, and shy. At play, everyone sat as students and automatically called on me to be the teacher and Yvonne to be the mother who cooked and disciplined.

I relished the sound of silence and spent hours reading or writing. Yvonne said silence drove her nuts and forced her to yell, scream, or do something to break it. Yet in the midst of all the pranks Yvonne pulled in church and Sunday school, we were all still learning.

Yvonne, thank you for the sisterhood we've shared. You're a big part of my life story.

David: David, you were our teacher in the primary (ages seven to nine) and junior (ten to twelve) classes in Sunday school. For a brief period, you were also my teacher at Sister Betty's school. You planned to take us on a journey through the entire Bible because you desired to make us living Bibles, so that if in the future we were imprisoned for our faith and denied access to our Bibles, we would have the Bible in our hearts. Your plans were cut short when your father, Pastor Eddie, was assigned to the United Brethren Church in Bowen's Content before we completed the junior class, and I don't recall seeing you since. I do remember that church was never the same after you left. We missed you terribly.

We remember the Bible lessons you taught us because even now, being much older and reading them for the umpteenth time, my mind still goes back to the first steps I took with you in studying the Bible. My former Sunday schoolmates and I speak of you often and the impact you had in shaping our lives. We remember that one Sunday in the middle of the David and Bathsheba story when you broke down and wept uncontrollably in front of us. You shared how Bible David, the man after God's own heart, sinned terribly but always repented sincerely, asking God to wash him with hyssop, to create a clean heart and renew a right spirit within him (Psalm 51).

That was such a powerful, sacred teaching moment of a repentant heart before God. Not one of us moved. There wasn't one giggle from a giggly bunch of kids under twelve. Not even Yvonne dared to move that morning. We were all touched and stirred in our hearts, and even though we couldn't explain why, we felt like crying too. To this day, Yvonne still recalls this moment with such reverence. Your tears were the most powerful lesson I learned in Sunday school, because it was unplanned—it went straight from your heart to God's and to ours. It taught us to repent and be humble in the light of God's Word and in his presence.

That moment impacted our lives more than any lesson could. Take pleasure in knowing that most of your students—now living in England, Canada, the United States, and various other countries—have found their way back to God and the church because you made us living Bibles. As we get older, we understand better why you broke down that morning: *"For the good that I would I do not: but the evil which I would not, that I do"* (Romans 7:19) and, *"For all have sinned, and come short of the glory of God"* (Romans 3:23).

> For the grace of God that brings salvation has appeared to all men, teaching us that, denying ungodliness and worldly lusts, we should live soberly, righteously, and godly in the present age, looking for the blessed hope and glorious appearing of our great God and Savior Jesus Christ, who gave Himself for us, that He might redeem us from every lawless deed and purify for Himself His own special people, zealous for good works. (Titus 2:11–14, NKJV)

To start a Bible lesson one Sunday, you asked, "What is an oasis?" No one volunteered an answer. I knew the answer, and you knew that I knew. You could tell from the grades I got in my Sunday school workbook. I was too shy to bless the Sunday school offering and rarely answered questions. "Bev, what grade are you in at school?" you asked.

"Grade four."

"You're in grade four and don't know what an oasis is? What's a mirage?"

I knew the answer to both questions but was way too shy to answer, and I secretly vowed that one day I would somehow tell you that an oasis was a fertile spot in the desert, and a mirage was an imaginary pool of water that people saw in the desert.

Where you left off, the living Word continued. The church I attended held Sunday school on Sunday mornings before the main service. But the Church of God close to my house held their Sunday school on Sunday evenings after dinner. As I hurriedly washed up the dishes and got ready for the seven o'clock movie at the Capri theatre in May Pen, followed by the Talk of the Town, Blue Gardenia (Blue G), Sunrise Inn, or Tempo City nightclubs—depending on access to a ride or featured guest band or artist—I would constantly hear the teenage students saying their memory verse out loud: *"Remember now your Creator in the days of your youth, before the difficult days come, and the years draw near when you say, 'I have no pleasure in them"* (Ecclesiastes 12:1, NKJV). It seemed as if this was the only verse they repeated each Sunday evening as I got ready to run off with Dolsie to May Pen. I knew that couldn't be the case, but it's all I can remember, as it burned in my memory and felt directed at me.

It's strange how Sweet Breeze was speaking to me at home, at school, at church, and even at play, yet I would come to Sunday school saying in my heart that God didn't know I existed. It's stranger still that I said in Sunday school that if God ever called me, I would do better than King Saul and King Solomon, yet I ran to the nightclubs, hiding and hoping to drown out his voice, only to hear him loud and clear, over and over, telling me he did not bring me to Canada to go to the nightclubs. Through it all, God remained faithful, making sure I prayed every day and night, or rather just before dawn, when I arrived home from the nightclubs—Thursday night to Monday morning—just in case I should die from the burnings. Even while screaming, "God, see what happens to someone when you don't know them!"

Now, to answer your questions: What is a mirage? What is an oasis? A mirage is not only an illusion in the desert or sea, but it's something unattainable, that elusive thing I left church to chase in the nightclubs and never found.

An oasis is not just a fertile place in the desert, but it's also Sunday school, and it's the Church in this world. It's Sweet Breeze accompanying me not only to find firewood but also to find my way through life.

I bet you're wondering how on Earth I know your middle name is Livingstone. Well, I peeked in your Bible one Sunday during Sunday school. You not only made us into repentant Davids but also into living stones in the process. I even remember the day you taught me in Sister Betty's school, when you placed each child on your knee to help them read. I remember how when my turn ended, I didn't want to get down.

I recall the Sunday morning when you gave Doreen Grant the doll that I desperately wanted and thought I should have gotten for perfect attendance all year. I also remember the hot and bright Sunday morning when I showed up to Sunday school dressed in my father's sunglasses, calling myself Kool Kat. I sat in the front pew with my legs crossed and my hands clasped about my knees, looking very cool in my shades. The class thought I was cool too, but you didn't agree. You asked me to hand over the sunglasses, and I refused. You picked me up and carried me to your father's adult Sunday school class. I wanted to be in my own class, and since your dad called my friend a spirit, I didn't want to be anywhere close to him. On the way, I wriggled and tried to get away. I almost got away when my wriggling forced you to stop and put me down. Realizing I wasn't winning, I turned to you in one of my rare brave and bright moments and asked, "Do you think you're my daddy?" A look of shock registered on your face at such impudence coming from me. You took me straight to Pastor's class and reported to him why I was there and what I had just said to you.

He said, "She said what?" I had to spend my Sunday school hour with Pastor and his class. That was no fun. So now we're even.

And the funny part of this episode is that I would have been in so much trouble at home if my father knew I had not only taken his sunglasses to church but also had the nerve to mouth off to you. As I said, that was a rare and brave moment indeed. I think I got the Kool Kat idea from Tony the Tiger or the Esso put-a-tiger-in-your-tank commercials. Thank you for helping to shape me into a Bible person and for helping shape your students into Bible people.

ENDNOTES

1 Gaither Vocal Band, "Satisfied," Spotify, track 8 on Gaither Vocal Band – Reunion, Spring House Music Group, 2009.

2 Isaac Watts (1752), "We're Marching to Zion," HymnSite.com, accessed July 6, 2023, https://www.hymnsite.com/lyrics/umh733.sht, public domain.

3 Watts, "Marching to Zion."

4 William F. Sherwin (1869), "Sound the Battle Cry," Hymnary.org, accessed July 6, 2023, https://hymnary.org/text/sound_the_battle_cry_see_the_foe_is, public domain.

5 Jester Hairston,, "Mary's Boy Child," performed by Harry Belafonte, An Evening with Belafonte, RCA Victor, 1956..

6 H.L. Gilmour (1885), "The Haven of Rest," Hymnary.org, accessed July 7, 2023, https://hymnary.org/text/my_soul_in_sad_exile_was_out_on, public domain.

7 Harry Clarke (1924), "Into My Heart," Hymnary.org, accessed July 7, 2023, https://hymnary.org/text/come_into_my_heart_blessed_jesus_come_in, public domain.

8 Albert Simpson (1905), "What Will You Do with Jesus?" Hymnary.org, https://hymnary.org/text/jesus_is_standing_in_pilates_hall_friend, public domain.

9 William Newell (1895), "At Calvary," Hymnary.org, accessed July 7, 2023, https://hymnary.org/text/years_i_spent_in_vanity_and_pride, public domain.

10 John Berry and Don Black (composers) and Andy Williams (performer), "Born Free," track 1 on Born Free, Columbia, 1967.

11 Henry J. Zelley, "When Israel out of Bondage Came," Hymnary.org, accessed April 8, 2024, https://hymnary.org/text/when_israel_out_of_bondage_came, public domain.